775

Applied Magic

Other books by Dion Fortune

Occult Study
Machinery of the Mind
The Esoteric Philosophy of Love and Marriage
Psychology of the Servant Problem
The Soya Bean
Esoteric Orders and Their Work
The Problem of Purity
Sane Occultism (to publish as *What is Occultism?* Weiser, 2001)
Training and Work of an Initiate
Mystical Meditations on the Collects
Spiritualism in the Light of Occult Science
Psychic Self-Defense
Through the Gates of Death
Glastonbury—Avalon of the Heart
The Mystical Qabalah
Practical Occultism in Daily Life
Applied Magic
Aspects of Occultism
The Magical Battle of Britain

Occult Fiction
The Demon Lover
The Goat-Foot God
Moon Magic
The Sea Priestess
The Secrets of Dr. Taverner
The Winged Bull

Applied Magic

DION FORTUNE
Introduction by Gareth Knight

WEISER BOOKS
Boston, MA/York Beach, ME

First published in 2000 by
Red Wheel/Weiser, LLC
York Beach, ME
With offices at
368 Congress Street
Boston, MA 02210
www.redwheelweiser.com

10 09 08 07 06 05 04
10 9 8 7 6 5 4 3 2

Library of Congress Cataloging-in-Publication Data

Fortune, Dion.
    Applied Magic / Dion Fortune.
            p. cm.
    Originally published: London: Aquarian Press, 1962
with new Introd.
    Includes index.
    ISBN 1-57863-185-8 (pbk : alk. paper)
    1. Occultism. I. Title.
BF1411 .F554   2000
133—dc21   00-040893

Printed in the United States of America
BJ

The paper used in the publication meets the minimum requirements of the
American National Standard for Permanence of Paper for Printed Library
Materials Z39.48-1992(R1997).

CONTENTS

INTRODUCTION
by Gareth Knight

APPLIED MAGIC is a collection of articles culled from Dion Fortune's *Inner Light Magazine* which was published from October 1927 through August 1940. Its columns were largely filled by Dion Fortune, herself. In its columns some of her great works, such as *The Mystical Qabalah,* first saw the light of day. It also contained many shorter pieces, written at the spur of the moment to meet a deadline, but which deserve preservation within the covers of a book. Hence this collection and its companion volume, *Aspects of Occultism.*

Dion Fortune's vision of occultism was a very practical one, and as she explains in her chapter, "The Occult Way," it is one based upon life experience. She had little time for a life-denying style of mysticism that looks down upon the outer world as an arena from which to try to escape. There were plenty of high-minded ineffectuals on the esoteric scene in her day, and indeed at one point she gave up a series of afternoon lectures because they were attended solely by nice-minded gentlefolk of the leisure class. The species is largely extinct through economic forces these days, although the attitude lives on in other social guises.

While it may seem to be a counsel of perfection to try "to obtain mastery over every aspect of created life," which was her idea of a Master, the way toward to such a state was not by withdrawing from life but rather by seeking to live it more abundantly. If the object of created life is for the human spirit to express itself within the worlds of form, through a process of personal spiritual evolution, it is hardly likely to be achieved by turning away from natural life. Thus the Path of the Hearth-fire, as she called it, involving the responsibilities of family life, was a sound and effective part of any initiate's training.

This might be gathered from those historical characters whom she considered to have been, if not Masters in life, then

upon the verge of becoming such in their last incarnate personality. Of these she cited Socrates, a wise man but a very
down to earth one, likened to Silenas, a follower of Dionysus's
drunken rout; Thomas Erskine, a lawyer and champion of
human liberty in the face of conservative reaction against the
French Revolution and the American War of Independence,
and also an early champion of animal welfare, but lampooned
as "Sir Ego" by his opponents; David Carstairs, a contemporary idealistic middle class young man who devoted himself to
youth work before meeting his death on the Ypres salient in the
World War I. None of them were ascetic gurus of the withdrawn kind.

In practical terms of our esoteric aspirations in the here and
now, the key element is one of motive, and as Dion Fortune saw
it, the one great disqualification from going very far along the
occult path was because, finding life too difficult, we want to
escape forever from its problems.

In "Some Practical Applications of Occultism" she gives a
very succinct résumé of just what training upon the occult path
involves. Fortunately, most of the veils of secrecy that she had
to put up with are no longer the barrier they once were, and
some of the credit for pulling them down rests with people like
herself and Israel Regardie, as she goes on to discuss in "The
Occult Field Today." Of the more popular revelations of esoteric teaching, such as the Spiritualist Movement and Christian
Science, she had considerable experience at various times in
her life.

Her parents had been keen members of the Christian
Science church, and her mother, Jennie Firth, had for some
years been a registered healer within it. Not a great deal of this
rubbed off on Dion Fortune, in fact rather the reverse seems the
case, for in 1922 the Firths gave up Christian Science and
removed to Letchworth. There they became associated with the
garden city movement and the promotion of soya as a vegetar-
ian alternative to dairy products, with a certain amount of
mediumistic advice from their daughter, who had recently been
developing these capabilities.

Records of Dion Fortune's mediumship in one form or another exist to cover most of the time between 1921 and 1945. She felt that her own type of work in this direction was not quite the same as most spiritualist mediums however, and in 1929-1930, she wrote a series of articles in her magazine to say so, under the title of "Spiritualism in the Light of Occult Science." Some of this material appears in this volume under the heading of "The Inhabitants of the Unseen" in "The Three Kinds of Reality." This caused a certain amount of upset within spiritualist circles at the time, particularly in the light of a series immediately following, called *Through the Gates of Death*, which contained some criticism of the indiscriminate calling back of the departed. *Through the Gates of Death* (Weiser, 2000) is now once more available and its strictures would seem no more than common sense precautions to most intelligent spiritualists, while the earlier work, re-titled *Spiritualism and Occultism* (Thoth, 2000) now includes much of Dion Fortune's ancillary writing on techniques of trance as well as an account of her attempted rapprochement with the spiritualist movement in 1942, when she envisaged a united front against the forces of materialism in the post-war epoch. These ideals, it seems, were either unrealistic or somewhat premature, and hardly lasted into 1943 before foundering on entrenched positions of mutual distrust.

She also took notice of the New Thought movement, which made great strides in the inter-war period under various forms of positive thinking, with applications ranging from salesmanship to auto-suggestive healing. Israel Regardie had also been attracted in this direction, and his little book *The Art of True Healing* (privately published in 1937) was, in essence, an attempt to meld a modicum of occult practice with New Thought methods. Dion Fortune confined her own endorsement to respect for Coué's empirical methods of auto-suggestion, but felt that they did not go far enough.

What she found lacking was a buttress of esoteric philosophy, which she lists as a knowledge of the implications of reincarnation and karma (or destiny) and the progress and manifestation of the soul upon different planes beyond the physical. The means for gaining awareness of all this and implementing useful action was, according to Fortune, through the practice of occult meditation, preferably aided by Qabalistic symbolism and magical ritual methods.

The latter involve technical considerations that are by no means confined to the occult lodge, upon which she expands in her chapter "The Group Mind." As she says, this factor is exceedingly important to the understanding of many human problems—in which may be included racism, religious conflict, xenophobia and mob violence. It also has a positive side however, of *esprit de corps,* patriotism, civic pride, corporate worship, aesthetic experience in concert hall or theatre— indeed, the list of applications is endless.

We may at this point note her endorsement of Trotter's *Instincts of the Herd in Peace and War,* which obviously made a big impression upon her to judge from the number of times she cites it in various writings (although here she got its title slightly wrong!). Its major attraction for her was its criticism of Freud's assumption that to cause someone to fit better into contemporary society was not necessarily a cure, but might simply inflict them with the same neuroses as society. Trotter was a distinguished biologist rather than a psychologist or sociologist, and professionals in these newer disciplines gave him short shrift. His book touched a public nerve at the time of World War I, particularly for its unflattering assessment of the German group mind, but eventually it went out of print, and although it is an interesting document for the student of the history of ideas, is hardly worth hunting down nowadays for its esoteric content.

More specifically, considerations of the technicalities of the group mind lead naturally to occult dynamics, which Dion Fortune examines in "The Psychology of Ritual." This, together with the latter part of her chapter on "The Group Mind," provides a neat summary of the rationale of ceremonial. More of her occasional writings upon this line, with a commentary, have been collected as *An Introduction to Ritual Magic* by Fortune & Knight (Thoth, 1997).

"The Circuit of Force" as it appears here is but a taster of what was in fact a long series of articles that ran from February

1939 through August 1940. We have here a conflation of the first article and the last article, but that which lies between has had to wait almost sixty years before appearing once again in its fullness, with a commentary, as *The Circuit of Force: Occult Dynamics of the Etheric Vehicle* by Fortune & Knight (Thoth, 1998). What we have here, however, gives some important indications as to the way her mind was working. She cites, for example, Jane Harrison's *Prolegomena to the Study of Greek Religion* as an important source, and also Sir John Woodroffe's *Principles of Tantra* as means of recovering what she calls "the Lost Secrets of the Mysteries."

Jane Harrison was a very remarkable woman who, in late Victorian times, forced her way into the exclusive male preserve of academic classical studies and kicked over the Olympean apple cart with a deep analysis of the Orphic and Dionysian roots of ancient Greek religious practice. Her book was published in 1903 and still remains in print. In the 1930s it had a profound effect upon Dion Fortune, who adapted some of the material for her own Rite of Isis, featured in her novels *The Sea Priestess* and *Moon Magic,* to say nothing of her semi-public performances at a converted church called the Belfry in West Halkin Street.

Dion Fortune's interest in tantra derives from her very fruitful association with the academic Bernard Bromage, whose university extension lectures she attended, along with her husband, in 1936. One thing led to another and from being Bromage's "star pupil" by the end of the following year they were jointly hosting a prestigious series of occult/literary discussion evenings. These were attended by well-known figures of the day, such as Christina Foyle (of the famous bookshop), and novelists and writers, such as Elliott O'Donnell, Marjorie Bowen, Berta Ruck and Claude Houghton.

In his academic work at this time Bromage was translating some Hindu tantric texts. These considerably interested Dion Fortune, who saw parallels with some Western traditions, not least with the supposedly discredited theories of animal magnetism. It is interesting to find in her private library exotic texts such as *Private Instructions in the Science and Art of Organic Magnetism* by Miss Chandos Leigh Hunt, privately published in 1884 in a lockable binding of gold velvet.

All this was the background to *The Circuit of Force,* which a later generation of Society of the Inner Light alumni viewed with a certain amount of nervous suspicion. It is to W. K. Creasey's eternal credit that he managed to include some of it in this volume of collected essays.

"Three Kinds of Reality" appears to be a conflation of some extracts from "Spiritualism in the Light of Occult Science" with some of Dion Fortune's occasional attempts to expound elements derived from *The Cosmic Doctrine.* The latter script, received by her between 1923 and 1925, was an exposition of metaphysical principles that owed something of its terminology to her first mentor, Theodore Moriarty (elements of which can in turn can be found in Blavatsky). However, in the hands of Dion Fortune and her contacts, they are transformed into a vast, but succinct, overview of spiritual solar logoidal evolution, with a cosmic background expressed in quasimathematical or geometrical terms.

The closer to earth element of this article comprises a description of various inhabitants of the unseen, human and nonhuman as perceived or conceived by Dion Fortune. The human includes the souls of the departed together with phantasms of the living, while the nonhuman includes the angelic and the elemental.

In the original text of "Spiritualism in the Light of Occult Science" she went on to cover nature spirits, demons, and projected thought forms, but these are covered in this book by an article titled "Non-Humans," a term which has a very wide definition in this context, for it covers "every sort of sentient intelligence which is not at the time incarnated in a human body."

This includes discarnate human spirits of the rarer kind, known as the Masters or Inner Plane Adepti. To her way of thinking, the ability to make this level of contact differentiates the work of the occultist from that of the spiritualist. That is to say, the spiritualist contacts the personality of a person recently deceased before that personality has moved on to what in esoteric terms is called the Second Death.

According to esoteric teaching favoured by Dion Fortune, the Spirit will then either project another personality into physical life or remain focused within the Higher Self upon a higher plane, the Higher Self being the accumulated evolutionary experience of all previous personalities. It is such that form the Guides and various grades of Inner Plane Adept or Master, or Initiates capable of functioning consciously in this way between physical incarnations. She goes so far as to say that the occultist is forbidden by the conditions of his training from making contact with the lower levels of what she calls the "living dead." This is the work of the spiritualist movement, whose mission is toward the general public as a means of demonstrating the existence of life beyond the grave, whereas the work of the occultist is upon a more specialised and withdrawn front.

The ability to contact the higher types of discarnate human consciousness brings with it congress with various nonhuman beings, some of which she has mentioned in her previous article: various types of elemental, various types of angelic beings. It can also on occasion bring about conscious contact with the demonic, for there can be fallen angels, just as there can be thwarted or twisted elementals, and criminally deviant human spirits. This brings us to the much vaunted sphere covered by her chapter "Black Magic."

She points out that there is far less of this about than might be assumed from the effusions of popular novelists, and by extension into other media of entertainment, or journalists seeking a sensational story to help sell a paper. Nor should we forget the subconscious projections of the ultra-righteous indulging in a hellfire version of old maid's insanity.

There is no more difference between white and black magicians than there is between altruistic and corrupt politicians, businessmen, or cops. The techniques across the spectrum of vice and virtue in any discipline are broadly the same—what makes the distinction is the motivation. In the esoteric sphere there is also the cosmic law that "like attracts like" which, on the one hand, can lead the aspiring soul toward the heights through contact with inner guides and helpers, and on the other, attract degraded inner entities to drag the erring soul into a negative spiral that can lead ultimately to self-destruction.

As Dion Fortune says, black magic is not a thing that any normal person would study or wish to pursue, but a certain knowledge of the pathologies of one's field of interest may not go amiss. In this respect, fiction may well be the best approach, but the highly entertaining occult blood and thunders of the paperback market are generally the works of ill-informed occult outsiders.

Dion Fortune wrote very much from the heart in this respect when she was conducting a review of occult novels for her magazine:

> The established writer who takes occultism for his theme only too often appears to have the most cursory knowledge of his subject. Moreover, it is curious to note that almost invariably the occult experiments that are described end in failure and everybody returns to normal life with a sigh of relief. They are afraid to carry to its logical conclusions the thesis which has attracted them sufficiently to cause them to undertake the labour of writing some seventy-five thousand words.
>
> Equally unfortunately, the author with a genuine knowledge and practical experience of occultism usually makes a lamentable failure when he turns his attention to fiction. His efforts are generally amateurish, inept and trite in the extreme. All the characters are cut out of cardboard with long propaganda speeches issuing from their mouths in solid blocks of platitudes. The person who, as I have done, essays the task of making a general review of occult fiction has a wearisome and nauseating task to perform.

So wearisome indeed did she find it that she never completed it, confining her remarks to just one writer, Algernon Blackwood, with his novels *The Centaur, Julius le Vallon,* and *The Bright Messenger* singled out for special mention, together with his books of short stories: *John Silence, Incredible Adventures,* and *Pan's Garden.* Her only other reference to fiction was in connection with books on Atlantis, when she mentioned Cutliffe Hine's *The Lost Continent,* Lord Lytton's *The Coming Race,* and Conan Doyle's *The Great Marracot Deep.* Although the one that she lauded as a neglected masterpeice was *Avernus,* the one novel written by her friend Mary Bligh Bond, who designed the dustcover for her own first occult novel, *The Demon Lover.*

In all walks of real life it is the exceptionally good or bad that makes the national news, whereas the vast field of actual human experience lies somewhere in between. In esoteric terms, a kind of grey hue characterises most casual attempts at magic. Dion Fortune defines this as "indiscriminate dabbling" and perceptively remarks that it is none the better for being accompanied by "a plentiful amount of specious piousness." Is there much point in calling a divine blessing down upon the distinctly dubious? Much of this takes account of nothing but personal desires, and promiscuous psychic dabbling forms no apprenticeship for serious esoteric work.

Serious esoteric work includes what she describes in "A Magical Body" as an imaginary personality. This article draws attention to the American author James Branch Cabell, who wrote a series of fantasy novels between 1917 and 1927 which have acquired a cult status, largely through his great erudition in matters of myth and legend, although his intentions were largely light-heartedly satirical rather than deeply transcendental.

He created a character called Horvendile who was also represented the author, and who was thus able to appear in his own fictions in this guise. Hence we have Dion Fortune's interest in the concept of a "Horvendile body," the magical equivalent of which is constructing a coherent imaginative form for one's own inner journeys. The first of the series, *The Cream of the Jest,* is the one that, to my mind, typifies Cabell at his best, and was followed by *Jurgen, Figures of Earth, The High Place, The Silver Stallion,* and *Something about Eve.* His irony is so subtle and pervasive that learned books and articles still discuss what he really meant and if he really meant it. However, Dion Fortune knew what she meant by a magical body, whatever the final critical assessment of James Branch Cabell may be. Like C. S. Lewis in *That Hideous Strength,* he seems to be capable of knowing enough about occultism to pass muster as a thought- provoking writer about it, without necessarily getting very involved himself.

Dion Fortune's review of "The Occult Field Today" dates from 1933. She had, by now, more or less established herself after a long struggle as Warden of her own Fraternity. The date of this article is important, for it marks the time when she and her husband met and became friends with Israel Regardie, recently arrived from the Crowley entourage in Paris, with his first books in process of publication. They were present at Regardie's initiation into the Hermes Temple of the Stella Matutina in Bristol, and put him up for the weekend at their hostel in Glastonbury.

All this came to grief when Regardie, not at all impressed with what he found, determined to do something radical and public about it. He denounced the Golden Dawn culture as he found it, and set about publishing all the Order's papers. All this is part of another story, but it destroyed Dion Fortune's standing with a Golden Dawn organisation for the second time, although peace was made once more in 1940, when she worked for a time with Maiya Tranchell-Hayes, who had been her mentor in the Alpha et Omega temple in 1919. This had apparently now ceased functioning and Maiya rather looked upon Dion Fortune and the Fraternity of the Inner Light as a last hope to keep the Golden Dawn Tradition going. She had recently, in despair, buried all her old regalia at the bottom of her garden, which, however, being on a cliff top, fell to the beach below through coastal erosion some years later, causing a six day wonder in the press.

It may have been Maiya Tranchell-Hayes, along with Brodie Innes and Mina MacGregor Mathers, whom Dion Fortune cites as being "reliable people" she knew who had "actually seen" the celebrated cypher manuscripts that were said to have brought about the founding of the Hermetic Order of the Golden Dawn. Dion Fortune's impressions of this organisation are somewhat mixed. In her view it had obviously seen better days, although she was in no doubt about the power that resided behind its foundation.

"The Occult Field Today" is an important article, not only in relation to Dion Fortune studies, but for the light that it throws upon other major players in the field of occultism in her day. Her assessments of MacGregor Mathers, Aleister Crowley, Israel Regardie, and the Besant-Leadbeater school of what she calls "Neo-Theosophical literature" make fascinating reading, together with her analysis of what makes an occult organisation an effective instrument of spiritual and metaphysical power.

This includes some form of inspired writings about which a nucleus of students can form, among which she is not afraid to cite her own *The Cosmic Doctrine*. This was a "received communication" dating from 1923–1925, although not published until after her death. At the time of writing this article, she was still only part-way through her major work, *The Mystical Qabalah*.

As to the works of others, she accords great importance to Blavatsky's *The Secret Doctrine* and also to MacGregor Mathers's rituals of the Golden Dawn. While many of her generation considered that their power would be destroyed through their publication, this has evidently not proved to be the case, as they obviously remain a source of great fascination for succeeding generations and revivalist groups. It is a little odd to see that Dion Fortune remains somewhat doubtful about the writings of Rudolf Steiner, although these, too, must rank as major works in the corpus of modern occultism. It has to be said that he has not been flattered by many of the translations of his work, although this may have improved over the years.

In her sections on "Subversive Elements in the Occult Movement" and "Occultism and the Underworld," she takes up various issues that were raised in her book, *Psychic Self-Defense* three years earlier, and in part of her series of 1920s articles for *The Occult Review* that were published in volume form as *Sane Occultism* (to publish as *What is Occultism?*, Weiser, 2001). The section titled "The 'Jewish Peril'" is very apposite when one takes account of the time it was written, when persecution of the Jews in Nazi Germany was just beginning to get under way. The quotation marks in the title are important as indicating that she regarded this idea as completely spurious.

Her article is probably generated in reaction to a book published in 1930 under the anonymous authorship of "Inquire Within" titled *Light-Bearers of Darkness*. It was a paranoid construction, followed up in 1936 with *The Trail of the Serpent*, convinced of a world plot leading to world domination organised by international Jewry, using the occult movement as its means of subversion. The author, billed as "for some years a Ruling Chief of the Mother Temple of the Stella Matutina of the R.R. et A.C." was Christina M. Stoddart, who seems plainly to have been in need of some psychological help. One can only say that if any world conspiracy seeks to utilise the organising capabilities of esoteric societies then the world can rest safe in its bed, for most have considerable difficulty in organising themselves, let alone cooperating with each other in some grand subversive design.

However, in the light of history there is a dark side to all of this, and the occult interests of Heinrich Himmler and the S.S. suggest that it was another kind of force altogether that was intent upon world domination, and not one that felt much empathy with the Jews. We find some pretty sweeping generalisations in Dion Fortune's brief excursion into the matter—not the least her opinion of the organising abilities of the Russians—but she plainly has her heart in the right place.

The concluding "Esoteric Glossary," although within the Dion Fortune tradition, is largely the work of Margaret Lumley Brown, a natural clairvoyant of remarkable abilities who gradually took over Dion Fortune's role after the latter's death in 1946. She continued as a major force within the Inner Light until 1961, when she was gradually pensioned off. Her story, and much of her writing and the fruits of her mediumship can be found in *Pythoness* (Sun Chalice, 2000).

CHAPTER I

The Occult Way

THE Mystic Way that leads to Divine Union is so well known that it is often forgotten that there is another Path, seemingly totally different in route, that leads in the end to the same goal. We are so accustomed to hear the renunciation of the world and the abnegation of the self set up as the only true Path of the soul which seeks the Highest, that we hardly dare whisper that there may be another Path—the Path of the mastery of manifested existence and the apotheosis of the self.

There are two ways in which God can be worshipped; we can worship Him in unmanifested Essence, or we can worship Him in His manifested form. Both ways are legitimate, provided that in worshipping the manifested form we do not forget the Essence, and in worshipping the Essence we do not confuse it with the manifested form, for these things are the sin of idolatry, which consists in a wrongly-placed emphasis.

The mystic seeks to worship God in essence. But the essence or root of God, being unmanifest, eludes human consciousness. The mystic, then, in order to conceive the object of his worship, has to transcend normal human consciousness. It is not possible to know the inmost nature of a state of existence unless we can enter into it and share, in some measure at least, its experience. The Mystic, then, has for his task the freeing of his consciousness from its habitual bondage to form. It is to this end that the ascetic discipline is directed, killing out the lower in order that the higher may be set free to unite with God and thereby know Him. The Way of the Mystic is a way of renunciation till he breaks all the limitations of his lower nature and enters into his freedom; nothing then remains that can withhold him from God, and his soul flies upwards to enter the Light and return not again.

But the other Path is not a way of Renunciation, but a Way of Fulfilment; it is not a breaking away from the path of human destiny, but a concentration and sublimation of that destiny. Each soul which takes that Path lives through its own experience every phase and aspect of manifested existence and equilibrates it, spiritualises it, and absorbs its essence.

The aim of those who follow this Path is to obtain complete mastery over every aspect of created life. But when we say mastery, we do not mean the mastery of a slave-owner over his slave. Rather do we mean the mastery of the virtuoso over his instrument; a mastery which rests upon his power to adapt himself to its nature and enter into its spirit and so draw forth its full capacity of interpretation. The adept who has gained mastery over the Sphere of Luna interprets the message of the Moon to the world and shows forth her powers in equilibrated balance. The kingdom ruled by the Master of the Temple is no absolute monarchy. He does not obtain that mastery in order to make thrones, dominions and powers serve himself, but in order to bring to them God's message of salvation and call them to their high heritage. He is a servant of evolution; it is his task to bring order out of chaos, harmony out of discord, and reduce unbalanced forces to equilibrium.

The Vedanta teaching of the Eastern Tradition clearly distinguishes between the devotion to the Unmanifest God, the spiritual essence of creation, and the manifesting aspects, or gods. "Identify the self with the partial aspects, which are the Yoginis, and the various Powers, (Siddhis) are attained. Identify the self with the Maha-yogini Herself, and man is liberated, for he is no longer man but Her. ... With what a man should identify himself depends upon what he wants. But whatever it is, he gets the Power if he but wills and works for it." (*World as Power*, *Power as Reality*, by Woodroffe.)

What ought a man to want? That is the next question

we have to ask ourselves. The answer to this depends entirely upon the stage of evolution we have arrived at. The soul has to complete its human experience before it is ready for Divine Union. It must pass the nadir of the descent into matter before it can come on to the Path of Return. We are not ready for the Mystic Way until we are approaching the time of our freedom from the Wheel of Birth and Death; to try and escape from that Wheel prematurely is to evade our training. Like the racing yacht, which fails to round the outermost marking-buoy, we are disqualified; we have not fulfilled the conditions of liberation, which command that we shall shirk nothing and leave behind us only that which we have mastered, equilibrated, and outgrown.

It is a false teaching which bids us eradicate from our natures anything which God has implanted there, as false and foolish as ham-stringing a spirited thorough-bred colt because it is wild and unbroken. The love of beauty, the vitalising urge of clean, normal, healthy instinct, the joy of battle, we should be poor creatures indeed without all these. God gave them to us, and we may presume that He knew what He was about when He did so. Who are we to judge His handiwork and condemn that which He found good?

What God's law forbids is the abuse of these things, not the use for the purposes for which they are intended. The Path of the Hearth-fire gives a far sounder and more effectual discipline of the instincts than the hermit-caves of Thebes, with their ascetic tortures and self-mutilations, doing violence to Nature and outraging God's handiwork.

Frightened by the Elemental forces when he meets them unpurified and unprepared, the ascetic flees from what he believes to be temptation. It is a far sounder policy to equilibrate the warring forces in our own nature until we can handle our unruly team of instincts and make them draw the chariot of the soul with the power of their untiring speed.

The day will come for each one of us when we shall be freed from the Wheel of Birth and Death and enter the Light to return not again; if we try to put aside the Elements and their problems before that day dawns we are shifting our helm for the homeward course before we have rounded the marking-buoy; we are like the man who buried his talent in the ground because he was afraid of it. Our Lord will not thank us for our misplaced devotion to an unripe ideal, but call us unprofitable servants.

The key to the whole problem, like so many others, lies in the doctrine of reincarnation. If we believe that all human achievement has to be accomplished in one life and that at the end of it we shall be judged, we are liable to be stampeded into an idealism which we have not yet attained by a process of natural growth. Freedom from the Wheel, the abandonment of matter, Divine Union—these will come for all of us in due course of evolutionary time, for it is the aim of evolution to bring us to them, but that time may not be yet, and we are very foolish if we allow another, however advanced, to judge for us where we stand upon the ladder of evolution, and decide what is to be our next step. Let us have the courage of our convictions and follow our own deeper promptings. If our urge is to worship God in His glorious manifestation, let us do it wholeheartedly; therein lies the way of attainment for us. This does not mean the unleashing of the impulses; the Dance of Nature is an ordered and rhythmical movement, we must not break from our place in the living pattern or we will spoil it. We must work with Nature for Nature's ends if She is to be our Mother. Here is discipline enough for any soul.

If, on the other hand, our promptings are towards a withdrawal on to the Mystical Path, let us ask ourselves honestly whether we are following that Path because the call of God in our hearts is so strong, or because we have found life so difficult that we want to escape for ever from its problems.

CHAPTER II

Some Practical Applications of Occultism

WHEN I first came to the study of Occult Science, it was extremely hidden and secretive. The various open societies that existed were either purely exoteric and elementary, or else they were really quite bogus. So it was difficult to know where to look for any real teaching. Consequently, unless one were psychic one was completely debarred from any knowledge. But this is no longer so in the same degree, and the problem remains for many people, do they want the occult teaching or not? We are so accustomed to think that in order to have any practical knowledge of occultism one must go apart from the world, and it is not practicable for the vast majority of people to follow that path at all. That meant that a very great many people who could have had great help from this teaching were debarred from pursuing its study, which I think is a pity. When I was training it was a strenuous affair altogether. The more I see of it, the more I feel that the work of the adept is one thing, and the general giving out of the teaching is another. The feats which are done by the trained gymnast are entirely beyond the scope of the ordinary man; but nevertheless, the same exercises on which the gymnast is trained, only not carried to the same extreme pitch, keep the ordinary man strong and fit when practised regularly. So I think it is with Occultism. If you want to be an adept and do the strong feats of Magic, you are equivalent to the gymnast, and this means a very strenuous training. But I think the next application of this work will be the bringing of the teachings, so that they are available for people not able to leave all, whose Karma holds them to daily life. It is interesting to note that at the time when the recrudescence of occultism began in the West—about 1875—three movements had their inception:

Occultism, the Spiritualist Movement, and Christian Science, with New Thought as its offspring. These are three distinct lines dealing with occult forces. The occultist bases his work on tradition and generally uses ceremonial. The spiritualist is approaching the same ground, but has no tradition and bases his work on experiment. The Christian Scientist has no tradition or experiment, but bases his work on the hypothesis of the powers of the mind. Spiritualism and Christian Science are rule-of-thumb procedures. If one studies the healing movement of Christian Science one sees that it has a very good method, but its practitioners seldom can explain it. Occultism is the scientific basis of all these movements and can explain the phenomena of these different modes of experience and practice. In that its value lies. Christian Science and New Thought do yield valuable fruits, but they give no explanation that a thinking person can accept, and yet they get their results. Therefore find that basis, and do not away with the valuable results. I maintain that in the esoteric doctrines we get an explanation of so much in life that everybody would be the richer for having them given. Life is a very different matter if we have a clue to its meaning. Without this we are like leaves blown in the wind, we do not know where we are or where we are going; we are blind and wandering as best we may, groping our way, with no guarantee that we do not fall over a precipice. But if we take the esoteric doctrines, then we see ourselves as part of the great whole.

We see our place in Nature, we see whence we have come and where we are going, and we see our relationship to the Cosmos, and the whole of life opens up. That is what eso-teric science can give—a very broad, profound and practical application of occultism. My experience with many esoteric scientists is this—they make a sort of intellectual study of it, but they do not apply it to practical problems. They are more or less engaged in research work, in studying symbol systems, the Qabalah, etc., but except as a means for divination these studies are for them of no practical applica-tion to life. Moreover these divinations are very spurious on the whole and tend to demoralise people's outlook on life. If something good or bad is going to happen to a person shortly, what good does it do to tell them so? But they can find the explanation of things in an interpretation of life. When we study the esoteric teachings of evolution, we see a tremendous vista opening up before us. And of course the belief in reincarnation is implicit in occultism, as is that in thought-transference. There we have, I think, one of the most illuminating teachings that can possibly be given to the problems of life. What can any being do in one life to earn either Heaven or Hell for ever? Surely the teaching of reincarnation is a more reasonable one—the going out and returning again, and going out once more into incarnation for further experience. That is to my mind a very wonderful concept of existence—that behind us stretches a long chain of incarnations. We do not remember them because the memory chain is broken, but they are there, and the Divine Spark is the core of each one of us, round which experience has built up a whole; this constitutes the temperament and capacities of each one of us. That concept gives us a very deep philosophy of life. If the fortunes of life are blind hazard, then indeed we are most miserable. But if we see that the broad outlines of the spiritual experiences that life brings us are determined by our own soul, we shall begin to see how to take things.

Then comes another question—the great esoteric doctrine of the invisible planes of existence. These teachings tell us that what the five senses see or contact does not constitute the whole of existence. This exoteric science can confirm, by means of the microscope, etc. But the occultist goes further and says there is a whole kingdom of mind and spirit as well, which you do not see with your physical senses. In these live the great Forces which actuate life and its circumstances. In it you will find the key to conditions of life on the physical plane, and you will never find it anywhere else. Such people as Coué are manipulating these invisible forces successfully. If we understand these conditions, we shall be free, we shall then be able to work with these forces and manipulate them ourselves. But we can manipulate them only within very definite limits. Christian Science sets no limits; but if we watch the results they obtain, we can see that there are limits. There are certain things you are wise not to meddle with. The occultist does not try to dominate Nature, but to bring himself into harmony with these great Cosmic Forces, and work with them. You can see an illustration of this if you watch the Thames bargees pushing off when the tide is on the turn; they are taking advantage of their knowledge of the tides, and the river does the rest. With us in life, we should have the same knowledge and wisdom. We ought to understand these natural laws of the Unseen. They are *natural* laws, and there is nothing spooky about them. We can make life a very different thing if we do understand them. Of course, there are certain conditions we must accept, that are the fruits of Karma; but I do not want you to take Karma in the crude way in which it is sometimes put forth. It is not a question of murder for murder, that if you steal from a person in this life, that same person will steal from you in the next. It is not as simple as that. It means that something in your nature has got to be realised and changed so that you shall be in harmony. As long as that particular factor is in your nature, it will precipitate a similar sort of trouble in your life. Errors of intention, deliberate wrong-doing, are usually paid for in future lives; you may get away with it in this life—we have all seen the wicked flourish like a green bay tree—but the effect of that goes on, it is put down to your account, and in due time you have got to pay. But payment is always in spiritual values. You learn that you have got to make certain adjustments, and when you have done this, the pressure eases up, and you are free. So point by point we gain character and equilibrium. We win our freedom by learning the lessons life forces on us; and if we refuse, they become more and more drastic. When people have arrived at a certain degree of development, they are more sensitive and have more spiritual force, and so their problems are more acute. The soul may have decided to go rapidly on, and brings down in a concentrated form all the Karma due. Trouble seems always to come down on this soul, and through an incarnation of trouble the soul is purified, and then the next incarnation opens up free of these conditions. A single incarnation does not furnish us with a clue, but leaves us with a sense of injustice; but if we see all our past lives stretching out, we see differently. We should always look at things in the light of three lives. And we can achieve our purposes in three lives too. We are making the conditions for our next life now, though in the present we have to take all or part of the Karma left from our last one. Some people say, "Surely one life is trying enough." But there is another way to look at it. If we average out our troubles against the long aeons of all our lives, they take on a different proportion. A great sense of freedom comes to the soul when the actual realisation comes that the "I" is going on, and that this incarnation is but an incident in its career. We cannot give anybody that freedom by simply explaining the logical grounds; but a sudden realisation comes of something that has been before, and this causes a great alteration of life's values. Again, if we inspect our life's problems we may find it may be because we are working things out rapidly and developing fast. We say: "This is the material condition that afflicts us, therefore we needed it, and we must learn the lessons it came to give". We try to interpret the spiritual significance of this experience. Let us develop our souls by meditation on it. When the soul has acquired this quality or learnt the lesson that it needed to learn, then the Karmic burden is lifted. When people tackle their conditions they do not change until the freedom is won. We think we would be happy if only certain things were changed; but no, the conditions are in ourselves, and would only bring other similar conditions back. When I was working in a nerve clinic we saw this happen over and over again. The same sort of trouble kept recurring in the same life. There was one woman who had been attacked by tramps three or four times in her life. This does not happen to everyone in the ordinary course of things. Or again, a woman may be continually falling under the power of a bully and be treated with cruelty—first a father, then a husband, and then in her work. We see one particular form of trouble recurring again and again in one person's life. There must be something which determines the recurring experience. If we, most of us, look back through our own lives we can see this to some extent at least. There must be some prominent factor in our own make-up which draws from the invisible forces. The only way to deal with these is by changing your character by meditation, by building thought-forms or by deliberately destroying what we call the thought-forms which are the channels of the undesirable things towards you. These are the practical applications of Occultism, and we do not need to be adepts to apply these. We are making thought-forms one way or the other all the time. Our thoughts not only influence us, they form channels of ingress and attract the corresponding forces in the Cosmos itself. If you surround yourself with hate-thoughts, you will be attracting a sort of Cosmic hate to yourself. The occultist has a system of labelling these forces, he works all these things out. We have such a system in the Qabalistic Tree of Life and the beliefs underlying it can be very valuable in life, they teach the tremendous power of mind and the strict limits in which it works, with which we can do so much. These doctrines should leaven thought more and more. The Theosophical Society has done a big work in this way, but its appeal has been chiefly to the unorthodox and the rebel. This is a great loss, because these teachings should be and can be presented in such a way that they do not estrange the trained mind, which in pure science is indispensable. Modern physics is coming completely round to the occult teachings. The things that Blavatsky said and was laughed to scorn for, are now becoming a matter of pure physics. There are great applications of these things which must be made. They should be applied to Sociology, to the administration of the prison and the asylum, where the thought-forms set up re-infect people unless we neutralize them. We can consider its practical applications to medicine, of which it has the only real keys. If you deal with man as body only, it is very unsatisfactory. Equally, if we take the orthodox view and deal with man as a spirit only, we are not doing him justice. Auto-intoxication and sin are different. Man is a fourfold being, and you must deal with him as such. You must discern on which level the trouble originates. The life forces of the spiritual level are the real keys to the whole problem, and these life-forces are translated through the intellect and the understanding and brought down the planes.

These are some of the esoteric teachings by which anyone can profit. I think the great need of occult secrecy is mainly past, but some is still necessary. Partly because a group-mind is necessary for some forms of practical occultism, and this has to be conserved, and not dissipated as is done if a thing is common property and knowledge; and also to safeguard individuals against popular prejudice. Madame David-Neel, in her books about Tibet, has told us that there is no secrecy about the *teachings* of the Lamas and the inner wisdom there. The things that *are* kept secret are the practical methods of training their students. She herself in her books has given out many teachings which are important keys to the understanding of many occult doctrines. There are no mysteries about the teachings, but only about the practical methods, with which people could do harm. So we see that the practical work of occultism can be done only by trained minds and requires a high degree of training; but the principles can be most valuable and the more these are given out the better.

CHAPTER III

The Group Mind

THE term Group Mind is sometimes used loosely among occultists as if it were interchangeable with Group Soul. The two concepts are, however, entirely distinct. The Group Soul is the raw material of mind-stuff out of which individual consciousness is differentiated by experience; the Group Mind is built up out of the contributions of many individualised consciousnesses concentrating upon the same idea.

Let us take a concrete instance to make this clear. During the height of his popularity Marshal Joffre visited England and was accorded a great ovation. While driving from his hotel to the Mansion House to be received by the Lord Mayor his car passed through many streets. Individuals recognized him and stared, but no demonstration was made. But when he came to the crowded Mansion House crossing, policemen held up the traffic, saluting; the crowd saw that something was afoot; he was recognized, his name passed from mouth to mouth, and in a moment there was a wave of wildest enthusiasm. Self-contained, placid people were lifted and carried away by the wave of excitement, and found themselves shouting and waving their hats like maniacs. Note the difference between the behaviour of the crowd when it functioned as a crowd from the behaviour of isolated individuals, however numerous, who merely stared with interest, but displayed no emotion.

This incident brings to mind another Mansion House incident very illustrative of crowd psychology and the group mind. Many years ago Abdul Hamed, the detested Sultan of Turkey, visited England. He too was received by the Lord Mayor and drove to the Mansion House. Exactly the same scenes were repeated but with a different emotional content.

He drove in safety through the crowded streets, individuals staring open-mouthed at the notorious visitor, but making no demonstration; but when the traffic was held up for him at the Mansion House crossing and the crowd recognized him, from those quiet, sober, middle-aged City men there went up a howl of execration like the cry of a pack of wolves, the crowd surged forward as one man, and it was with the greatest difficulty that he was saved from being dragged from his carriage.

Which of those individual City men, unadventurous clerks content with their desks, would have assaulted the aged and august Abdul Hamed single-handed? Yet when caught up in the wave of crowd emotion they were capable of making a savage attack amid a babel of animal snarlings. For the moment something like an obsessing entity took possession of the souls of all and each; a vast Something, of a character which was not the sum of the mass of the individual souls, but vaster, more potent, more fiercely and vividly alive and conscious of its impulses. Yet at ordinary times the thronging crowds at the Mansion House crossing go each their own way, absorbed in their own thoughts, indifferent to, oblivious of their neighbours. What was it that turned this mass of hurrying, indifferent units into a united band uplifted by the enthusiasm of an ideal, or an organism capable of dangerous violence?

The key to the whole situation lies in the direction of the attention of a number of people to a common object about which they all feel strongly in the same way. Direction of attention to a common object without emotion does not have the same effect. The electric signs of Piccadilly Circus, though crowds stand and watch them, do not cause the formation of a group mind.

With these data to assist us, let us consider the problem in its occult applications. What is this strange oversoul that forms and disperses so swiftly when a number of people are of one mind in one place? For an explanation we must consider the theory of Artificial Elementals.

An Artificial Elemental is a thought-form ensouled by

Elemental essence. That essence may be drawn directly from the Elemental kingdoms or it may be derived from the magician's own aura. A thought-form built up by continual visualizing and concentration, and concerning which a strong emotion is felt, becomes charged with that emotion and is capable of an independent existence outside the consciousness of its creator. This is a very important factor in practical occultism, and the explanation of many of its phenomena.

Exactly the same process that leads to the formation of an artificial Elemental by a magician takes place when a number of people concentrate with emotion on a single object. They make an artificial Elemental, vast and potent in proportion to the size of the crowd and the intensity of its feelings. This Elemental has a very marked mental atmosphere of its own, and this atmosphere influences most powerfully the feelings of every person participating in the crowd emotion. It gives them telepathic suggestion, sounding the note of its own being in their ears and thereby reinforcing the emotional vibration which originally gave it birth; there is action and reaction, mutual stimulus and intensification, between the Elemental and its makers. The more the crowd concentrates upon its object of emotion, the vaster the Elemental becomes; the vaster it becomes, the stronger the mass suggestion it gives to the individuals composing the crowd that created it; and they, receiving this suggestion, find their feelings intensified. Thus it is that mobs are capable of deeds of passion from which every individual member would shrink with horror.

A mob Elemental, however, disperses as rapidly as it forms because a mob has no continuity of existence; the moment the stimulus of a common emotion is removed, the mob ceases to be a unit and reverts to heterogeneity. That is why undisciplined armies, however enthusiastic, are unreliable fighting machines; their enthusiasm evaporates if it is not continually stimulated; they split up into their component parts of many individuals with diversified interests, each activated by the instinct of self-preservation. To build up a group mind of any endurance some method of ensuring continuity of attention and feeling is essential.

Whenever such continuity of attention and feeling has been brought about, a group mind, or group Elemental, is formed which with the passage of time develops an individuality of its own, and ceases to be dependent for its existence upon the attention and emotion of the crowd that gave it birth. Once this occurs, the crowd no longer possesses the power to withdraw its attention or to disperse; the group Elemental has it in its grip. The attention of each individual is attracted and held in spite of himself; feelings are stirred within him even if he does not wish to feel them.

Each newcomer to the group enters into this potent atmosphere, and either accepts it, and is absorbed into the group, or rejects it, and is himself rejected. No member of a group with a strong atmosphere, group mind, or Elemental, (according to which term we prefer), is at liberty to think without bias upon the objects of group concentration and emotion. It is for this reason that reforms are so hard to bring about.

The vaster the organization that needs reforming, the harder it is to move, and the stronger must be the personality that attempts the task. Yet once that forceful personality has begun to make an impression he speedily finds that a group is gathering under his leadership, and that this in its turn is developing an Elemental, and the momentum he has originated has begun to push him along. When he flags in his leadership the movement he created forces him forward. The solitary individual may turn aside and pause in moments of doubt and discouragement; not so the leader of a strongly emotionalized group; as soon as he slacks his pace he feels the pressure of the group mind behind him and it carries him forward during his hours of weakness and darkness. It may also, if his scheme has been unwisely conceived, carry him away and dash him to pieces on the rocks of a misjudged policy, a policy of which he would have seen the unwisdom if he had considered the matter rationally.

There is no stopping the momentum of a movement which is moving along the lines of evolution. The group mind of the participants forms a channel for the manifestation of the forces of evolution, and the momentum developed is irresistibie. But however potent the personality, however vast the resources, however popular the catch-phrases, if the movement is contrary to cosmic law it is only a matter of time till the whole group rushes madly down a steep slope into the sea. For in such a case it is the very momentum that is worked up which is the cause of its destruction. Give a false movement enough rope and it will always hang itself, falling by its own weight when that has grown sufficiently top-heavy to overbalance it.

This factor of the Group Mind is an exceedingly important key to the understanding of human problems, and explains the irrationality of men in mass. There are some very interesting books upon this subject, notably, *The Psychology of the Herd in Peace and War* by Wilfred Trotter, and *The Group Mind* by William McDougal. These will well repay study for the light they throw upon the problems of everyday life and human nature. The occultist carries the practical application of the doctrine of group minds much further than does the psychologist. In it he finds the key to the power of the Mysteries. Considered with an understanding of crowd psychology, it becomes obvious that the method of the Mysteries and the secret fraternities of all ages is based upon practical experience of its facts. What could be more conducive to the formation of a powerful group mind than the secrecy, the special costume, the processions and chantings of an occult ritual? Anything which differentiates a number of individuals from the mass and sets them apart forms a group mind automatically. The more a group is segregated, the greater the difference between it and the rest of mankind, the stronger is the group mind thus engendered. Consider the strength of the group mind of the Jewish race, set apart by ritual, by manners, by temperament and by persecution. There is nothing like persecution to give vitality to a group mind. Very truly is the blood of martyrs the seed of the Church, for it is the cement of the group mind.

It is for this reason that the secrecy of the Mysteries will never be entirely abrogated. However much is given out, something must always be kept in reserve and secret, because this something which, unshared with others and the focus of the attention of the group, is the nucleus of the group mind, the focus of its attention; it is to the group mind what the grain of sand is to the pearl forming within the oyster. If there were no grain of sand there would be no pearl. Remove that which differentiates the initiate from the rest of men and the group mind of which he forms a part will fall to pieces.

The potency of ceremonial, physically performed, does not rest only in its appeal to the entity invoked but also in its appeal to the imaginations of the participants. An adept, working alone, will work a ritual in picture consciousness on the astral without moving from his meditation posture, and this ritual will be effective for the purposes of invocation. But if he wants to make an atmosphere in which the development of his pupils will advance as in a forcing-house, or if he wishes to raise his own consciousness beyond its normal limitations, transcending his own will power and unaided vision, he will make use of the powers of the group Elemental developed by ritual.

This group mind, or ritual Elemental, acts upon the participants in the ceremony in exactly the same way as the mob emotion acted upon the peaceful City men when they saw Marshal Joffre. They are lifted out of themselves; they are more than human for the moment, for a group Elemental, formed of the appropriate emotion, is just as capable of raising consciousness to the level of the angels as of lowering it to the level of the beasts.

When our emotion goes out strongly towards an object, we are pouring out a subtle but nevertheless potent form of force. If that emotion is not a mere blind outpouring, but formulates itself into the idea of doing something, and especially if that idea causes a dramatic mental picture to rise in the mind, the outpouring force is formulated into a thought-form; the mental picture is ensouled by the out-poured force and becomes an actuality upon the astral. This thought-form itself now begins to give off vibrations, and these vibrations, by the law of the sympathetic induction of vibration, tend to reinforce the feelings of the person whose emotion gave rise to them and to induce similar feelings in others present whose attention is directed to the same object, even if they have hitherto been dis-interested onlookers.

It will be seen that the theory of the group mind is now being associated with the doctrine of auto-suggestion as formulated by Baudouin, and these two established psycho-logical concepts are extended by association with the eso-teric concept of telepathy. Take these three factors together and we have the key not only to the phenomena of mob psychology, but also to the little realized power of ritual, especially ritual as it is performed in an occult lodge.

Let us consider what happens when such a ritual is per-formed. All present have their attention rivetted upon the drama of the presentation of the ceremony. Every object within the range of their vision is symbolic of the idea that is being expressed by the ceremony. No circumstance that can heighten the concentration and the emotion is neg-lected. Consequently a highly concentrated and highly energized group is built up.

As we have already seen, when one thinks of any object with emotion force is poured forth. If a number of people are thinking of the same object with emotion, their attention concentrated and their feelings exalted by the ritual of the ceremony, they are pouring into a common pool no in-considerable measure of subtle force. It is this force which forms the basis of the manifestation of whatever potency is being invoked.

In religions where the gods or the saints are freely repre-ented in pictorial form, the imaginations of the worshippers, are accustomed to picturing them as they have seen them represented; whether it be the hawk-headed Horus or the

Virgin Mary. When a number of devout worshippers are gathered together, their emotions concentrated and exalted by ritual, and all holding the same image in imagination, the outpoured force of all present is formed into an astral simulacrum of the being thus intensely pictured; and if that being is the symbolic representation of a natural force, which is what all the gods are intended to be, that force will find a channel of manifestation through the form thus built up; the mental image held in the imagination of each participant in the ceremony will suddenly appear to each one to become alive and objective, and they will feel the inrush of the power that has been invoked.

When this process has been repeated regularly over considerable periods, the images that have been built up remain on the astral in exactly the same way that a habit-track is formed in the mind by the repeated performance of the same action. In this form the natural force remains permanently concentrated. Consequently subsequent worshippers need be at no great pains to formulate the simulacrum; they have only to think of the god and they feel his power. It is in this way that all anthropomorphic representations of the God-head have been built up. If we think for a moment we shall see that the Holy Ghost is neither a flame nor a dove; neither is the maternal earth-aspect of Nature either Isis or Ceres or the Virgin Mary. These are the forms under which the human mind contrives to apprehend these things; the lower and less evolved the mind, the grosser the form.

Those who have a knowledge of the little understood aspects of the human mind, whether Egyptian priest, Eleusinian hierophant, or modern occultist, make use of their knowledge of this rarer kind of psychology to create conditions in which the individual human mind shall be able to transcend itself and break through its limitations into a wider air.

CHAPTER IV

The Psychology of Ritual

AT the Reformation the men who made the Anglican ritual did not understand the psychological significance of the Roman ceremonial. They saw it in its degradation as an empty channel, and they broke up the conduit because it was dry. Let us be wiser in our generation, and instead of breaking up the conduit, connect it up with the well-head.

There is a spiritual reality behind the forms of organized religion, and it is that reality alone which gives them their value. They are not intended to be a discipline to train the soul, nor even to be a means of pleasing God, but are designed to enable the Light of the Spirit to be brought to a focus in consciousness. If we understand the psychology of ritual we shall neither be in bondage to superstition nor in rebellion against empty forms. We shall realize that a form is the channel for a force, but it is not only the material substance used in a sacrament which is the physical channel for a force, but also the vivid pictorial image created in the mind of the worshipper by its ritual use.

It is to the power behind the symbol that we must look when we seek for the validity of the Church's forms. The outward and visible sign, be it cup or cross, is but the focusing point of attention which enables the worshipper to come into psychic touch with the form of spiritual force which is the animating life of that symbol. We must learn to look to psychology, not to history for an explanation of the significance of the Church's symbols and rituals. What is commemorated is not a mundane act, but a spiritual reaction, and it is only as we ourselves make that inner reaction that we share in the efficacy of the act which was its prototype. The crucifixion of Our Lord at the hands of Roman authority was but the shadow thrown on the material plane by the struggle that was going on in the spiritual world. It was not the spilling of the blood of Jesus of Nazareth that redeemed mankind, but the outpouring of spiritual power from the mind of Jesus the Christ.

The symbolism which commemorates His death causes us to concentrate our attention on the Sacrifice of the Cross and the work it accomplished for mankind. The racial subconsciousness of Christian peoples is profoundly imbued with that ideal, and when we contemplate the symbol universally associated with it, we waken the subconscious train of ideas which rouses deep racial memories. The ritual which causes a congregation to concentrate its attention is making use of the group-mind. It is well known that the group-mind, under the influence of rage or fear, is capable of panics and lynchings of which the individual members composing that crowd are quite incapable; so it is with the impulses of the spiritual life. A congregation is an organized crowd with its attention rivetted by appeals to all five physical senses upon a single focus—the sacrifice of the Mass, and the group emotion thus engendered is able to lift the group mind to heights which the individuals composing that congregation are incapable of achieving unaided.

It must not be thought that such an explanation of the psychological aspect of the power of the Eucharist is intended in any way to detract from the recognition of its Divine aspect; it is solely intended to show the manner in which the spiritual forces operate on the level of mind. If we wish to understand the *modus operandi* of the spiritual forces, we must distinguish between the spiritual and the mental. It is the confounding of the two types of psychology which leads to so much misapprehension.

The power of God has to be embodied in a concrete idea if it is to be apprehended by the untrained human mind. Hence the necessity for the Incarnation, which presented God to man in a form which he could grasp.

So the sacraments of the Church are incarnations or embodyings in form of primary spiritual truths, too abstract to be apprehended by the untutored mind. By means of their pictorial symbolism the mind is enabled to contemplate that which, unaided, it could never conceive. This contemplation enables it to link itself on with the spiritual potency which performs the work shadowed forth by the priest on the physical plane. Thus linked in thought, the spiritual power pours into the soul and accomplishes its divine work.

There are therefore three aspects to a sacrament—the formless power of God translated from the abstract to the concrete by Our Lord; secondly, the symbolic ritual which reminds us of that particular function of Our Lord's work; and thirdly, the image formed in our imagination. When this last forms in consciousness, the circuit is completed, and Our Lord has put us in touch with God.

CHAPTER V

The Circuit of Force

IT is not easy to convey Eastern thought to Western readers because the dictionary equivalent of the terms employed is very far from being their significance in mystical thought. It is well known to those who have penetrated beyond the Outer Court in these matters that there is a special use of language, a *double entendre*, as it were, which is made use of whenever questions of practical procedure are under discussion, lest the "once-born" should discover the short cuts to the secret places of the soul. It is both right and necessary that this precaution should be used, and it will be observed in these pages; for these short cuts are effectual psychological devices, and can be made use of by the undedicated as well as the dedicated, and if they are employed by persons with unpurified and undisciplined minds can prove unfortunate for others as well as themselves. I would be the last to deny to an adult the right to burn his own fingers if he so desires, but think it best to withhold from him the means of raising conflagrations in other folk.

Another difficulty in the way of conveying Eastern thought to Western readers lies in the fact that the attitude towards life of East and West is entirely different; this is strikingly illustrated by the sacred buildings in the two hemispheres. In the West, the central emblem commemorates suffering: in the East it commemorates joy. The men and women conditioned to these emblems naturally evaluate the experiences of life differently. As Kipling truly said: "The wildest dreams of Kew are the facts of Khatmandu, and the crimes of Clapham chaste in Martaban."

The best approach to Eastern thought is through a classical education. The Greek and the Hindu would have no difficulty in understanding each other; each has the same concept of Nature and the same regard for asceticism as a means to an end and not as an end in itself. Eastern thought, however, has penetrated far more deeply into natural religion than the Greeks had the capacity to do, and the Mysteries of Dionysus and Ceres are but pale shadows of their Eastern prototypes.

It may be not without value in this connection to examine what is known concerning the origin of the Greek Mysteries. It is believed, and for the grounds for this belief the reader may turn to the pages of *Prolegomena to the Study of Greek Religion* by Jane Harrison, that when Greek national religion began to lose its hold on an increasingly enlightened people, an attempt was made, by no means unsuccessfully, to provide a rendering of it acceptable to thinking men by borrowing the method of the Egyptian Mysteries and expressing it in terms of the older, earlier Greek Nature cults that preceded the highly poetized tradition of the bright Olympians. These old Nature cults still lingered in the out of the way parts of Greece, in the islands, and in the mountains, and the Mystery myths show clearly that their originators knew this fact, for in them the god comes down from the mountains or the goddess takes refuge in the island. It must be clearly recognized that these Mystery myths are not by any means primitive material, but very sophisticated material indeed, being the work of scholars and mystics of a highly civilized era seeking in the ancient traditional roots of Greek religion for untapped springs of inspiration. It was exactly as if a modern Englishman sought inspiration from Keltic or Norse folk lore. No doubt the initiates of the Mysteries were regarded as pagans in their own day.

There is another fact, which, though known to specialists along this line of study, is unrealized by the majority of writers on mysticism, and consequently by the majority of their readers. It will no doubt be a surprise to many to learn that Indian initiates believe that the inspiration of their Mysteries came originally from Egypt. The relevant data may be found in the works of Sir John Woodroffe (Arthur Avalon). See, in particular, the extract from Panchkori Bandyapadhyga on p. XXIV of Vol. II of that author's *Principles of Tantra*.

It follows, then, that those who have been initiated in the Western Esoteric Tradition, and have taken those grades that draw their inspiration from Greece and Egypt in addition to the better known alchemical grades, will have no difficulty in understanding much in Eastern thought that is obscure, or even obscene to the ordinary student.

The practical applications of such teachings, valuable as they could be as a corrective to our insularity, are, however, far from easy to attain. It is frequently said that Yoga as taught in the East is impractical in the West because the Western conditions of life are utterly unsuited to it, and the Western attitude utterly unsympathetic. I can only repeat this standard advice yet again. The student should on no account attempt the practical work of advanced Yoga unless he has the necessary conditions of mind, body and estate, for all these three play their part. Practical Yoga should not be done in any makeshift manner, but with proper care and attention to all the material conditions that are necessary for its achievement. If these are not available, it is inadvisable to make the attempt with substitutes. Among these necessities are the necessary number of properly trained persons in a properly equipped and prepared place that is secure from profanation. Again I emphasize that makeshifts are worse than useless. If you do Yoga at all, do it under proper conditions or leave it alone.

But despite these provisos and warnings, I think it worth while to write on the subject of Yoga because I feel that my training in the ancient Mysteries of the West has given me an insight into it that the average Christian does not possess. There have been a great many books written on the subject, their writers all frankly recognizing that Yoga in its original form is unsuited to the West, and one and all trying to present an adaptation of it that should be suitable; but one and all, so far as my experience goes, have thrown away the baby with the bath-water, and presented a version of that ancient science which is like a version of Hamlet edited by a rationalist who removed all reference to the supernatural. The result does not make sense.

The fact, however, remains that Yoga as it stands does not suit the West, and that if the mountain cannot go to Mahomet, Mahomet will have to go to the mountain if he wants to enjoy the delights of a high altitude. Our Western culture has bestowed many benefits in the way of physical sanitation, but the same cannot always be said of it in regard to mental sanitation, and a modification of its attitude is due, and overdue, as the psycho-analysts have long been pointing out.

In earlier writings I have tried to show the practical implications of the doctrine of Manifestation by means of the Pairs of Opposites, which is one of the most fundamental and far-reaching tenets of the esoteric tradition. Much of what I have had to say is so profoundly esoteric and so immediately practical that I have been obliged to adhere to the ancient method of myth and metaphor. These things are not for the profane, who would either misunderstand them or abuse them. Those who have eyes to see can read between the lines.

In this present context I will try to sum up the principles involved and bring the whole concept to a single focus; yet even so, such is its inherent nature, as in fact the nature of all manifestation, that my argument must needs move in a circuit, returning whence it started for its final explanation and application.

Manifestation takes place when the One divides into Two that act and react on each other. Manifestation ends when Multiplicity is resolved or absorbed back into Unity. The transition from plane to plane of manifestation takes place in the same manner. In order that any thing or factor shall be brought down from a higher to a lower plane, it is necessary to analyse it into the contradictory factors that are held in equilibrium in its nature. To do this, one imagines the opposite extremes of which it is capable and expresses them separately while retaining in consciousness their essential unity when in equilibrium.

Equally, if it is desired to raise any factor from a lower to a higher plane, one conceives its opposite and reconciles the pair in imagination and realization.

Any pair of factors, divided for the sake of manifestation, act and react upon each other, alternately struggling to unite and, in the act of uniting, exchanging magnetism, and then, their magnetism having been exchanged, repelling each other and striving to draw apart, thus re-establishing their separate individuality; then, this established and a fresh charge of magnetism having been generated, once again they yearn towards each other in order to exchange magnetism, the more potent giving off, and the less potent receiving, the charge. It must never be forgotten in this respect that relative potency is not a fixed thing, depending on mechanism or form, but a variable thing, depending upon voltage or vitality. Moreover, the charge passes backwards and forwards as an alternating current, never with a permanent one-way flow.

These are fundamentals of the concept, and they have their application to every aspect of existence. Ignorance of them, and our inveterate tendency to try and maintain the status quo whenever and wherever it is established, causes endless sterility, as needless as it is destructive and wasteful, and whose cause is utterly unsuspected.

An illustration will serve to show the far-reaching ramifications of the influence of this principle. Apply these concepts to the relationship of initiator and candidate, of leader and follower, of man and woman; then, having so applied them, re-read these pages and see if you can then see what is written between the lines.

But not only is there a flow of magnetism between the Pairs of Opposites, but there is a circulation of force between parts and the whole. Man is a perfect Microcosm of the Macrocosm; none other creature, so it is taught, shares this development. To the angels, the lower aspects are lacking; to the Elementals, the higher. In consequence of his manifold nature, man is in magnetic relationship with the cosmos as a whole, not merely with a limited or selected presentation of it. There is a flow and return between every aspect of our beings and characters and the corresponding aspect in the cosmos. Just as the chemical elements in our dense body are derived from and returned to the general fund of matter, so by the processes of metabolism, the psychic factors in our subtler bodies are neither static nor exclusive, but are maintained by a perpetual flow and return like a hot water circuit which flows from boiler to storage tank and back again by virtue of its own physical properties. If we are for any reason cut off from this free flow of natural force, some aspect of our nature atrophies and dies. Or if the flow is checked without being blocked, some aspect suffers starvation. There is a characteristic deadness when this occurs, readily recognizable in all the relations of life when once its nature is realized. If the initiator is not in contact with spiritual forces, he cannot pass them on to the candidate and so "fails to initiate." If the candidate brings no real depth of feeling to his initiation, he gives out no magnetism; and as magnetism can only be poured into a person who is giving it out,—a little understood, but far-reaching truth—that candidate receives no down-pouring of power and the initiation is ineffective. If a leader has not great principles to guide him but is a mere opportunist, his inspiration to his followers will consist in no more than a hope for a share of the spoils. If a man and a woman are not each in touch with Nature, they will have little to give each other that is of any vital value and so will soon part— on the inner planes, even if convention holds them together on the outer plane.

The operation of magnetic interchange in all its aspects can be cultivated and developed. In its subjective aspect it is developed by certain Hatha Yoga practices, which, though definitely dangerous if done incorrectly, are very valuable if done correctly. Without this development of the subjective magnetism and the acquirement of skill in its direction and control, it is impossible to operate either safely or satisfactorily the contacts with the corresponding reservoirs of magnetic force in the cosmos; but once some degree of development and skill has been attained, it is a waste of time to persevere with exclusively subjective methods.

Contacts with cosmic forces, however, are not things to be made at random, any more than contact with a lightning flash; therefore formulae are used to enable the mind first to contact and secondly to control the chosen cosmic force. These formulae can, in the case of experienced operators, thoroughly skilled in the art, be purely mental and consist of images in the imagination representative of the force in question. But only very highly developed people can obtain results by purely mental means, and for less developed people, the co-operation of others in group working is necessary. Solitary working soon becomes arid, wearisome, and unproductive of results, as every student of occultism can testify.

Nevertheless, unless there is solitary working, the operator becomes de-magnetised. Consequently we must accustom ourselves to the idea of a perpetual change of state, and alternation between subjective solitary working and objective group working. Not otherwise can we hope to maintain the sense of zest which tells us that the forces are flowing freely.

These things are the secret not only of magical power but of life itself in all its relationships. They are things of which even the most enlightened exoteric thought is entirely ignorant, and they are the real keys to practical occult work. They are the Lost Secrets of the Mysteries, secrets which were lost when an ascetic religion, though a valuable corrective to excess, destroyed the polarising opposite truth which alone could maintain it in equlibrium. It is the great fault of our ethic that it is incapable of realizing that one can have too much of a good thing.

When, in order to concentrate exclusively on God, we cut ourselves off from nature, we destroy our own roots. There must be in us a circuit between heaven and earth, not a one-way flow, draining us of all vitality. It is not enough that we draw up the Kundalini from the base of the spine; we must also draw down the divine light through the Thousand-Petalled Lotus. Equally, it is not enough for our mental health and spiritual development that we draw down the Divine Light, we must also draw up the earth forces. Only too often mental health is sacrificed to spiritual development through ignorance of, or denial of, this fact. Nature is God made manifest, and we blaspheme Her at our peril.

CHAPTER VI

The Three Kinds of Reality

UNLESS we realize the difference between the Cosmos and the Universe, we shall never achieve a true understanding of esoteric philosophy. This point is an exceedingly important one, for it marks the distinction between those who know how to interpret the symbol systems and those who do not.

The concept is not an easy one to grasp, but we will try to convey it as simply as possible, for many important practical points arise out of it.

For all practical purposes our solar system is a closed unit. The influences received by it from the other heavenly bodies change, if they change at all, in such vast cycles of time, that we are justified in considering them as constant so far as we are concerned. This solar system arose from a nebula, the planets being thrown off by the sun, and in their turn throwing off their attendant moons. We may therefore say, as regards our universe, "In the beginning there was a nebula."

But when we have said that, we have not disposed of the problem. Whence came the original nebula? That it was condensed out of the diffused matter of space, may be the answer to that question. But still we have not got to the beginning. Whence did the matter of space, whatever that may be, derive the inherent characteristics which came out in the process of its evolution? In fact, the very word evolution implies involution. Nothing can be unfolded which was not previously infolded. There must have been a phase of existence which preceded the unfolding of evolution, for evolution is not a continuous creation of something out of nothing, but a coming into manifestation of latencies.

We solve this problem, for the purposes of any reasoning

we may want to do, by positing the Great Unmanifest, the Root of All Being, which is really the metaphysical equivalent of X, the unknown quantity. In algebra, X enables calculations to be made with known quantities, but at the end we are none the wiser concerning its own nature than we were when we started. In metaphysics whatever we do not understand, we refer to this X, which is not only the Great Unmanifest, but also the Great Unknown.

The Unknown, however, is a relative term, and esotericists, or for the matter of that, evolutionists also, would not agree with Herbert Spencer that the Great Unknown is also the Great Unknowable. With the extension of human consciousness, either in the course of evolutionary development or by intensive methods, a great deal can become known which was hitherto unknown. In fact a great deal is known to the scientist, the philosopher, the metaphysician, that is a part of the Great Unknown so far as the average man is concerned; and much is known to the average man which is also part of the Great Unknown to a young child.

The Great Unknown, therefore, is not a thing in itself, but rather a relationship that exists, or perhaps more accurately, does not exist, between the Self and certain aspects of the Not-self.

The Great Unmanifest cannot be the Great Non-Existent. The Non-Existent just *isn't*, and that is all there is to be said about it. But the Great Unmanifest very much *is*, and to call it the Root of All Being is a very good description. It is only unmanifest so far as we are concerned, because we have not got, at our present state of evolution at any rate, any faculties or senses by means of which we are able to contact it. If an extension of consciousness takes place, however, by means of which we become conscious of an aspect of the Root of All Being which had hitherto been unperceived by us, then for us it is no longer Unmanifest, but has become Manifest.

Might we say, then, that manifestation takes place by means of realization? The actualities, which are the underlying noumenal essences of all that exists, never become manifest in that they become objects of sensory experience. But are our apprehensions limited to sensory experience? The psychologist says, yes. The esotericist says, no. No sensory experiences enabled Darwin to apprehend the law of evolution. His five senses may have enabled him to observe the innumerable phenomena on which his ultimate deduction was based, but it was a faculty quite distinct from sensory consciousness by means of which he finally grasped the nature of the underlying cohesion between the innumerable separate units which had passed under his observation in the course of his researches.

Is a formula which resumes a number of objective facts any less a reality than the facts themselves? Does its reality consist in the marks which as figures and letters represent it upon paper? Is it not a thing in itself upon its own plane? We need to disabuse our minds of the idea that only dense matter is real. There are many forms of energy which are not physical. Behind the physical reality there is a psychic reality, and behind the psychic reality there is a spiritual reality. To think in terms of matter only is a bad mental habit and gives a totally false outlook upon existence.

The psychic reality we may define by saying that it consists of the sum-total of the realizations, however, dim, that consciousness, however rudimentary, has achieved. Of the spiritual reality, we had best limit ourselves to saying that it consists of the as yet unapprehended Great Unmanifest, and that in it is the Root of All Being.

And even when a psychic reality is formed through realization, the spiritual reality is not done away with, but remains as the underlying essence which gives validity to the whole. For there may be psychic realizations which are not realities, but unrealities, because inadequate or inaccurate, and in them we may look for the root of Positive Evil.

It may well be asked, what practical consequences can there be for us in the work-a-day world as consequence of these fine-spun metaphysical subtleties? When we are bearing the burden and heat of the day, what does it matter to us whether there is a psychic reality as distinguished from the thing-in-itself, the spiritual reality? And would it ease our burden did we know?

It is upon such considerations as these that the whole structure of the practical application of mind-power rests; it is in the field of psychic reality that the reasonings and affirmations of Christian Science and the New Thought movement in general find their scope and derive their power. It is in the field of psychic reality that the adept and the magician work by means of the trained mind, for the plane of psychic reality is susceptible to mental manipulation.

THE INHABITANTS OF THE UNSEEN

Whoever contacts the invisible world, whether by means of his own psychism or by employing the psychism of another as a channel of evocation, has need of some system of classification in order that he may be able to understand the varied phenomena with which he will meet. Not all of them are due to the spirits of the departed; there are other denizens of the invisible world than those who have once had human form. Nor are all the phenomena due to the subconscious mind entirely subjective. Confusion arises when that which should be assigned to one division is allocated to another. It can be clearly shown that the explanation which is offered does not account for the facts. Nevertheless, the facts are not disposed of by showing the explanation to be fallacious. A correct classification would yield an explanation which can stand up to any impartial investigation and be justified of its wisdom.

The classification which it is proposed to employ in these pages is drawn largely from the traditional occult sources, and it is believed that it will throw light on certain experiences met with by psychic research workers. It is offered in a spirit of co-operation, as independent testimony to a common experience.

I. THE SOULS OF THE DEPARTED

Of all the inhabitants of the invisible worlds, the ones with which it is easiest for us to get into touch are the souls of human beings who have shed their outer garment of flesh, either temporarily or permanently. Anyone who is familiar with spiritualistic or esoteric thought soon become habituated to the idea that a man is not changed by death. The personality remains, it is only the body that is gone.

The esotericist, in his concept of the nature of departed souls, distinguishes between those who are going through the inter-natal phase, that is to say, who are living in the non-physical worlds between incarnations; and those who will not incarnate again. There is a great difference in capacity and outlook between these two types of souls, and many of the issues at present outstanding between spiritualism and occultism are undoubtedly due to a failure to recognize this fact.

The occultist does not maintain that existence is an eternal sequence of birth and death, but that at a certain phase of evolution the soul enters upon a series of material lives, and through the development made during these lives, it finally outgrows the mundane phase of evolution, becoming more and more spiritualized towards the end of this period, until finally it wins its freedom from matter and re-incarnates no more, continuing its existence as a disembodied spirit with a human mind. Mentality, the occultist maintains, can only be obtained through incarnation in human form. Those beings who have not undergone this experience have not got mentality as we understand it, with certain exceptions which we will consider later.

For the most part, it is the souls of the living dead who are contacted in the seance-room. Liberated souls go on to their own place and are not so easily reached. Only those return within range of the earth-sphere who have some business there. The discussion of this point would open up a vast field of interest which we cannot deal with at the moment. It must suffice to say that, as is well known to all workers in psychic research, there are souls of a higher type than those commonly encountered, who are concerned with the evolution of humanity and the training of those who are willing to co-operate with them in their work.

We may say, then, that the souls of the departed may be divided into three types: the souls of the living dead, who will return again to the earth-life; liberated souls who have outgrown earth-life and have gone on to another sphere of existence; and the liberated souls who, having gone on, return again to the earth-sphere because they have work to do therein. A recognition of these three types of departed souls will serve to explain many of the discrepancies we encounter between the statements of spiritualists and occultists. The occultist aims chiefly at getting into touch with the liberated souls for the purposes of specific work in which both he and they are concerned; for the most part, he leaves the souls of the living dead severely alone. Personally, I am of the opinion that he is mistaken in so doing. It is quite true that they can be of little assistance to him in his chosen work, but the normal companionship of the living with the dead robs death of most of its terrors and is steadily building a bridge between those who remain and those who have passed over. The occultist should certainly not invite the co-operation of the living dead as he would that of the liberated souls, for they have their own work to do; nor can he place as much reliance on their knowledge and insight as on that of those who are freed from the wheel of birth and death; neither has he any right to try to use them as he would Elemental spirits in the course of his experiments. Admitting these qualifications, however, there seems no reason why the occultist should not share in the interchange of amenities which is continually taking place across the borderline. After all, death is one of the processes of life, and the dead are very much alive and quite normal.

II. PROJECTIONS OF THE LIVING

The appearance of a simulacrum of a human being at the point of death is exceedingly common, and innumerable well-attested instances exist of its occurrence. It is not so well known, however, that it is possible for the simulacrum, or astro-etheric form, to be projected voluntarily by the trained occultist. Such projections, in proportion to the hosts of disembodied souls encountered when the threshold is crossed, are exceedingly rare; nevertheless they occur, and may be met with, therefore they must be included in any classification which aims at being comprehensive. Usually such a projected soul appears to be entirely pre-occupied with its own affairs and in a state of absorption which causes it to appear to ignore its surroundings. As a matter of fact, it most frequently happens that the disembodied spirit has its work cut out to maintain consciousness at all on the higher planes, and its self-absorption is that of the beginner on a bicycle. Occasionally communication may be established between such a projected etheric body and a group of experimenters, and very interesting results are obtained; but unless there is sufficient materialization to render the simulacrum visible to the non-psychic, the experiment will partake rather of the nature of telepathy grafted upon mediumship than of a true projection of the astro-etheric form.

Such visitants are neither angels nor devils but "human, all too human".

III. THE ANGELIC HIERARCHIES

The average Protestant has a very dim notion concerning the angelic hierarchies, the great hosts of beings of another evolution than ours, though children of the same Heavenly Father. The Qabalah, however, is explicit on this point, and classifies them into ten archangels and ten orders of angelic beings. Buddhist, Hindu and Mohammedan theology are equally explicit. We may therefore reckon that in this agreement of witnesses there is surety of testimony, and it may serve our purpose best to take for our guide that system from which Christianity took its rise—mystic Judaism.

We will not go into the elaborate classifications employed by the Jewish rabbis, which have their importance for purposes of magic but are not germane to our present issue. It is enough that we realize that there are divinely created beings of varying degrees of greatness, from the mighty archangel whom St John the Divine saw standing in the sun, down to the nameless heavenly messengers who have from time to time visited mankind.

Beyond the spheres to which are assigned the disembodied spirits of humanity dwell these heavenly beings, and in some high ranges of spiritual light the psychic or medium sometimes touches them. In the Vale Owen scripts there is much concerning them that is of great interest.

It is said by the rabbis that these beings are perfect, each after their kind; but they do not evolve, and it is noticeable that they are non-intellectual. One might almost call them divine Robots each strictly conditioned by its own nature perfectly to fulfil the office for which it was created; free from all struggle and inner conflict, but changeless, and therefore unevolving.

No angel, it is held, ever goes outside his own sphere of activity. The angel who has "healing in his wings" cannot bestow vision, nor the bestower of visions serve as the strong guard against the powers of darkness.

Esotericists make a fundamental distinction between angels and the souls of men. They say that the Divine Sparks, which are the nuclei of the souls of men, proceed from the noumenal cosmos, from the same plane whereon the Solar Logos has His being. They are therefore, of the same innermost nature as the Godhead. Angels, on the other hand, are created by the Solar Logos as the first of His created beings. They neither fall into generation, nor rise by regeneration, but remain in changeless but unevolving perfection till the end of the epoch.

The functions of the angels are diverse, and cannot be entered upon here in detail. They are, each according to his office and rank, God's messengers in things of the spirit, but they have no direct contact with dense matter. That office is performed by another order of beings altogether, the Elementals, who differ in origin and inmost nature from both angels and men.

IV. ELEMENTALS

Much confusion of thought exists concerning the orders of beings known as Elementals. They are sometimes confused with the spirits of men. Undoubtedly many happenings attributed to spirits are to be assigned to the activities of these other orders of beings. Again, they are not to be confused with the evil demons, or, to give them the Qabalistic name, the Qliphoth.

Elementals are the thought-forms generated by co-ordinated systems of reactions that have become sterotyped by constant and unchanging repetition. Some explanation is necessary to make this concept clear, and we shall understand it best if we survey the means by which elementals come into being.

Each epoch of evolution is constituted by the outgoing and return of a life-wave of living souls. These are referred to in esoteric terminology as the Lords of Flame, of Form, and of Mind. The present evolution will become the Lords of Humanity. Each life-wave develops its characteristic contribution to evolution. When the Divine Sparks which constituted the nuclei of the evolving souls of each evolution are withdrawn back up the planes and reabsorbed into the Kingdom of God, their work remains behind them in that which they have builded, whether it be the chemical elements evolved by the Lords of Form, the chemical reactions evolved by the Lords of Flame, or the reactions of consciousness evolved by the Lords of Mind.

Humanity, it is held, is evolving the power of co-ordinated consciousness, and the Lords of Humanity therefore hold the same relationship to the Lords of Mind that the Lords of Flame hold to the Lords of Form. These beings, however, of the three earlier life-waves, have passed out of range of the life of our earth, each group to its appropriate plane, and the Lords of Humanity are still absorbed in the task of building, and are not yet, save those few who have become Masters, escaped from the bondage of the material in which they work. Consequently, it is but rarely that any psychic save the higher grades of adept ever contacts any of these beings.

They have left behind them, however, as has already been noted, the forms which they built up in the course of their evolution. These forms, as psychics teach, actually consist of co-ordinated systems of magnetic stresses. Whenever any movement takes place an electric current is set up, and if the series of co-ordinated movements is repeated many times, these currents tend to make adjustments among themselves and become co-ordinated on their own account, quite independently of the physical forms whose activities gave rise to them. It is out of these co-ordinations that the Elementals are evolved.

We cannot go more deeply into this most interesting and intricate subject in the present pages. It is a matter for a separate study. Enough has been said, however, to indicate that although the ultimate product of the evolution of the angelic, the human, and the Elemental kingdom is to produce consciousness and intelligence, the origin of the three types of beings is entirely different, and so also is their destiny.

The Divine Sparks are the emanations of the Great Unmanifest, Ain Soph Aur, in the terminology of the Qabalists; the angels are the creations of the Solar Logos, and the Elementals are "the creations of the created", that is to say, they are developed out of the activities of the material universe.

Of the Elementals thus evolved there are many types. Firstly, the four great divisions of the Elemental spirits of Earth, Air, Fire and Water, known respectively to the Alchemists as Gnomes, Sylphs, Salamanders, and Undines. These really represent four types of activity arising out of four types of relationship. In solids, (the Element of earth) the molecules adhere together. In liquids, (the Element of water) the molecules are free-moving. In gases, (the Element of air) they repel each other and therefore diffuse to their uttermost limits. And in fire the essential property of its activity is to change plane, or transmute. The four kingdoms of primary Elementals, under their angelic kings represent the co-ordinated, purposive, and intelligent action of these four properties of matter—the mind-side of the material phenomena, to be precise.

This fact is well known to occultists, and they employ the mind-side of matter in their magical work. Consequently many of these Elemental systems of reactions have, as it were, been domesticated by adepts. Elementals thus domesticated become imbued with consciousness of a human type. These developed, (or initiated) Elementals are sometimes met with by psychics.

We are now trenching upon some of the most secret aspects of occultism, and not a great deal can be said; and even if it were said little of it would be understood save by those who were already well versed in esoteric science.

CHAPTER VII

Non-Humans

BY this term in this article we mean in a general way every sort of sentient intelligence which is not at the time incarnated in a human body—this includes those discarnate spirits who speak through mediums and those we call Masters or Inner Plane Adepti, not sharing in our human life, though human spirits, but we reckon them as non-human for purposes of classification. We will take the contact with beings who are not in physical bodies. We read a great deal about these contacts in medieval literature, so too have the ancients a lot to say, and to-day among the primitive tribes of the East and of the New World. Also there is a good deal about it in certain sections of our own folklore, especially among the Celts. The average Anglo-Saxon is content with one non-human only, and that is the Devil. So then we are dealing with a considerable body of testimony to the contact between human beings and non-humans, and there is no smoke without fire. So we have to consider. Are there such things? Is communication possible, and if so, is it advisable under any conditions or certain conditions?

Taking the broad question of other phases of evolution, there is no reason why there should not be other forms of existence than dense physical matter. To the untrained person, nothing is real but the material things he can bump into and fall over. But anyone with any experience in scientific work, knows that there are unseen forces of existence on the level next removed from dense matter, which we can get at with absolute certainty. Why should there not be others just a little further on? Are we to limit ourselves to that we can see, or are we to say, that there are more things in heaven and earth than are dreamt of in our philosophy?

We will take this for granted now to save our time, and go on to consider the nature of the non-humans. Esoteric Science teaches us that there are other lines of evolution as well as our own. Just as light and sound take up no space in our air, so these beings do not occupy space, have not got weight or mass, they interpenetrate matter and you might walk through one, as through a ghost. They are different modes of consciousness from ours. We might see a musician in raptures, in a state of rapture at what might sound to us a mere din, because his trained ear distinguishes the sounds. So there are these other modes of existence different from ours, and they interpenetrate ours. We contact these other modes of life only under three conditions. We have to begin to perceive in a different way; then we find that we are meeting with beings of a kind that we did not know existed, and it is a surprising experience for both. Secondly, we may come into contact with these other beings if there is someone about who is a materializing medium and who can exude ectoplasm. Thirdly, occultists who go in for such forms of work, by magical operations can invoke beings of other forms of existence into materialization. So then we see there are conditions by which we can contact them, but it is a process out of the normal for both parties. When a human being raises consciousness to the subtle planes, he is, as it were, a ghost to the inhabitants of that plane. Therefore when we do, we get a sense of danger, of things inimical to us; the reason being that these beings are afraid of us and on the defensive. It is different in the case of the initiated occultist, who goes out into the unseen with "letters of introduction", and there is a fraternal relationship. Then the consciousness of the adept moves out along well-known tracks with his credentials, and he no longer finds these planes antagonistic, he knows how to behave, and it is an entirely different matter. But these journeys are not things to be undertaken haphazard by anyone. We can give much offence to the beings of another plane and be pushed back forcibly. The question of communication between the two planes resolves itself into the change of the levels of consciousness on our side, or the assembling of a substantial form on the other side, and in both it is essential that both shall know what they are about and observe certain precautions.

And now what manner of beings are they who are thus contacted? First, there are living dead, those whom the Spiritualists usually contact when they reach the unseen. The Spiritualist movement was brought into being about the same time as the modern occult movement and Christian Science. Four big movements moved off in the last quarter of last century—Spiritualism; Christian Science and its allies, New Thought, etc.; the Theosophical Society under Blavatsky; and a general stirring and movement of life in the Western Esoteric Tradition itself, which is much less known. Each of these had its own work to do. The Spiritualists had for their work association with the human spirits of the departed who were still within the earth's sphere. They never did much outside that. Just as the occultist working on his contacts up and down a given ray, comes in touch with beings of his ray, so the Spiritualists work, and so their experience is limited. These beings are human Personalities. Most of you know that the human Personality endures for a while after the death of the body, going through a purgatorial experience, from there to a lower heaven to rest in a pleasant dream, then to the Second Death, the death of the Personality of this incarnation, including the lower mind, which is disintegrated; from this the Higher Self is set free and passes some time in the higher heaven before re-incarnating. The type that the spiritualist meets with are beings in the lower heaven; I do not think there is any sign of beings who are functioning in the Individuality. It is the function of the spiritualist movement to work with beings on these levels because its work was to break down the barrier between the living and the dead. The occultist, on the other hand, is forbidden by his conditions to have any dealings with the living dead. He opens up his contact with those of the human kind who have passed beyond the re-incarnating phase of evolution, and also with some other different forms of existence which are very interesting. So then the occultist finds that when he is able to function in his higher consciousness, he is coming across beings of quite different kinds ˙from himself. These are classified. We may take them as being the Elemental beings. They are quite different in kind from humanity. They have no Divine Spark, they will be disintegrated at the end of this evolution and cease to exist, unless they can develop within themselves a spiritual nature. These beings come into existence thus—Wherever you get a series of constantly co-ordinating actions and reactions, you get what we call "tracks in space", which remain; after the activities which gave rise to them have ceased. We can compare them to the swirling of the water in a stirred-up basin, after the stirring has ceased the swirls in the water continue for some time. These throughout nature are the basis of any beings and on this basis develop the possibilities of response to environment and memory. Thus we gradually get the difficult concept of the building up of consciousness out of natural phenomena. The Building Spirits, who thus operated in the first place the great natural phenomena when they were being created, are Angelic Beings. They withdraw up the planes, and leave the Elementary consciousnesses to carry on with the stereotyped mode of reaction. These remain and develop, and we call them "the creations of the created"— these lives called into existence not by God, but by God's creatures, who have no power to endow them with immortal life. Whenever you get a system in nature which reacts as a unit, a mountain, a dell, a wood, you have the same system of co-ordinated stresses in the background, and thus come the little nature spirits, or Devas, or gods of localities, which our ancestors worshipped. The same idea is at the back of different species of animals. If you have any knowledge of biology you will know there are very simple beings, uni-cellular, and the generalized consciousness of these may not have a single life under its control, but many. There are certain periods in its existence when there is only a green patch on some damp surface and this breaks up into innumerable little things; these live for a time in a free-swimming form, then they all gather together and form a large homogenous mass, called plasmodeum. What becomes of the consciousness as a unit in its free-moving form? Or take bees, the hive is the unit there, and not the bee. The unit might be called the bee-angel. We get these different curious units of consciousness evolved. Next, what is the logical outcome? Higher, more developed modes of nature forces. There is a very curious occult doctrine, that these beings, becoming more and more developed and coming more to resemble the types of consciousness with which we are familiar, become conscious that they are lost souls unless they can develop a spiritual nature. They seek as initiators those who have got a spiritual nature; the initiated man is the initiator of the Elemental being: Humans take them as pupils and help them to develop their "sparks" of individual consciousness. In return for this service the Elemental beings perform services for the magician. We read of these as familiar spirits. The writers on these matters were usually the priests, and being charged by the Inquisition to enquire into it, were usually a little prejudiced. But there is a certain relationship between people who understand the inner planes and beings of another order. And there is also an involutionary relationship, very often, between those people who are naturally psychic without training and quite spontaneously come into touch with other beings. The effect of this is seldom wholesome. It has the effect of unbalancing them. It is a too intensely stimulating contact. Elementals are of a pure type, composed of one Element only, whichever that may be, whereas a human being is a mixture of all. So they are too potent a stimulus to that one Element in our own being, which is very apt to throw a human being off his balance, lure him to follow it and abandon his human ways. He is "taken by the fairies", or what we should call a pathology. You can see the thought control withdrawing from the physical vehicle. They hear the call of the fairies, and only an empty shell remains, insane. When the magician invokes a spirit to individual appearance, he puts himself into a circle and draws a triangle outside it and causes the spirit to manifest in this; then he will do the banishing ritual and return it whence it came, to its own sphere. But he usually does this only for research work, or to help a pathology. We must draw the distinction between the serious research worker and the person who is out for experimenting. Nothing but harm is likely to result in this latter way.

What other forms of creatures are there? I have mentioned the Angelic Beings, the great Archons, the building spirits who built up the planes of nature in the time of other evolutions. There are all manner of very lofty spiritual beings whose mode of manifestation is in nature. They are classified in different ways. We talk about the heathen who worship many gods, but in every religion there is always the Being behind the gods, the Father of the gods, the Oversoul, a very abstract conception of a Being. The "gods" of any system are these natural forces, called the Archangels and Angels in the Hebrew system which we ourselves use. The spiritual beings have never had a material incarnation, have never descended into matter. The old tradition is that the choice was offered to the spirits whether they would remain on the inner planes, neither ascending nor descending, or descend to the depths of matter in order to rise higher than they had started from; and one lot chose one line, led by Adam, or rather Eve, and others chose the other. So the angelic hosts are our kin and if you go far enough back you find a time when men and angels were of one company. Thus it is possible under certain conditions to contact these angelic beings, but in most cases we do not contact the actual being, who is very vast; we contact his ray, his emanation. If you were sufficiently rich you could engage a great opera singer to come to your house and sing in your drawing-room; but if you had only enough for a wireless set, you could hear him on the air. When we invoke the Archangel Raphael we do not expect him to turn up in person, but we do expect to feel his force, his ray. It is the same with the visions of Christ that have been seen, the Vision Beautiful. It is not the actual being, but tuning in on the ray, though it is the same thing for practical purposes. We need to understand these things. We are not dealing with an actual anthropological form, but with modes of consciousness, and some are so different from ours that there is no analogy. We must not think of them all as fairy figures, they are consciousnesses which are quite incomprehensible to us.

In addition to all these, there is an innumerable host of thought forms, cast off from human consciousness, artificial Elementals deliberately made by human beings. These last for various lengths of time so that there is a legion of different types of beings, neither angels nor devils. The idea that all which is not physical is either divine or evil is not true. Non-humans are very much like humans, neither perfect nor omniscient, but evolving. A final point—the beings which the Qabalists call the Qliphoth. These are demoniacal, dwelling in the Kingdom of Unbalanced Force, which came into existence before equilibrium was established; different types of inharmony, reinforced by the mass of evil thoughts ever since. When you touch the Unseen, you are unlikely to touch the divine beings of any sphere without also touching the Qliphoth of that sphere. If you contact a Sephira you touch its unbalanced side also. You dare not open up a higher contact with any of these spheres unless you are able to hold down the lower. This is a great truth of the spiritual life. The initiated adept knows this. He always aims at the equilibration of these great forces. At the last, all the kingdoms of the earth and below the earth shall be redeemed. Our Lord went to preach to the spirits in prison to redeem them. They are simply misplaced force, which when returned to its proper place, ceases to be evil. The adept may not curse the devils he must replace them to equilibrate them. The adept never speaks of hell, but of the kingdoms of unbalanced force. The Tree of Life enables us to travel about on the thirty-two paths, which are distinct and well-trodden ways and the adept moves about among the Elemental beings with accuracy, and knows where he is; he can maintain his equilibrium.

What useful purpose does it serve to contact these forces?

First, it is sometimes necessary for the adept to open up these conditions in order to clear up something that has gone wrong with a soul. He may have to open a sphere to operate, like a surgeon, to bring into equilibrium and to return into its own sphere what has gone wrong. Also, he may operate the forces of a sphere in order to bring the concentrated forces of that sphere into his own being, so that he may work with it. Thirdly, it may be he has some special work to do which he can only carry out this way. In short, to bring harmony, to intensify his own nature, and possibly for other reasons. This kingdom is of varied nature. The conditions under which communication can be rightly done are rare; there should be a distinct turning off and on of the tap; but things can be effected by these means which are otherwise impossible.

Haphazard communication is more or less of a crime and the consequences can be disastrous. Then why not keep this knowledge secret? Because there is so much of it about that it is better, probably, to see what is going on. If you bump into things in the dark, it is better to have a light to see what is happening and to bring control. These forces exist. They can be dealt with. It is well to know this, as there is already so much knowledge about.

CHAPTER VIII

Black Magic

BLACK magic is not a thing that any normal person would study or pursue for its own sake, but it is hardly possible, and hardly advisable, to study the technical methods of occultism without giving consideration to the pathologies to which they are liable. Such popular attention as occultism receives is for the most part confined to its black aspect; revelations of this aspect can always command the kind of attention that is given to a street accident. Anyone who has any knowledge of occultism, however, is always struck by the fact that the would-be exposers never get their fingers on the real evil. They sense the evil, just as animals sense an abattoir, but they have no realization of the significance of the facts they record, nor any understanding of why the people concerned are doing such things.

The technique of black magic differs in no way from that of white magic; the same principles apply, the same methods are made use of; the same training in concentration is necessary; the difference lies in the attitude of the operator, the symbolism employed, and the powers contacted thereby; just as the same musical education is necessary to the conductor of a symphony orchestra or a jazz band. And even when we say that certain symbols and powers belong to the domain of black magic, we must make reservations, for these symbols may be used, and these powers evoked quite legitimately, just as dangerous risks are taken by surgeons upon occasion. One can safely say, however, that should any of these magical methods be exhibited to an audience, they can be unhesitatingly classified as black, because they cannot fail to arouse the baser instincts of the spectators, who are there for no useful purpose. There are also certain techniques of sex and blood magic which, though they may be harmless enough among primitive peoples, are certainly out of place among civilized ones, and are only resorted to for the sake of a debased sensationalism. To these we must add the deliberate evocation of evil; this is usually only performed for purposes of revenge. But there are certain types of persons with a natural streak of cruelty in their natures; these readily take to the evocation of evil for vengeful purposes, and having had experience of the results of this operation, develop a liking for it for its own sake and become cruelty addicts for the sake of the thrill it gives. Unless we recognize this peculiar trait in human nature, which is much commoner than is generally realized, and is distinguished by psychologists by the name of sadism, we shall never understand certain aspects of black magic, for it is in sadism that the key to these is to be sought.

The invocation of certain primitive types of natural forces, though not intrinsically black, is an operation that is very liable to go septic, and should only be done by experienced and dedicated operators working under laboratory conditions. It is an important part of the training of every adept, for when cosmic forces are invoked, they always come up in pairs, action and reaction being equal and opposite; but he would never dream of evoking the unbalanced or Qliphotic aspect by itself or for its own sake, that being too risky an operation. For practical purposes, when Elemental forces are handled, they are dealt with in their sublimated forms, Sekhmet, the Lion-headed fire-goddess, for instance, being a preferable form to Kali. These crude forms of force, however, have to be understood by the occultist or he will have trouble with them.

Anyone who makes a serious study of occultism has got to understand these things, and people are not to be branded as black because they study them; in fact they would be very superficial students if they did not; but anyone who makes a public exhibition or popular exposition of black magic most certainly stands condemned; for it is not necessary that anyone save specialists should be acquainted with these things, and it is better for the general run of mankind to leave them alone; for to dwell upon them tends to put one in touch with them, and unless one takes the precautions that the initiate takes when dealing with them, one is liable to infection.

One cannot divide magic into white and black by a clear-cut dividing line; there is what may be described as grey magic, which people embark upon out of ignorance or love of sensation. One must therefore recognize the grey variety, of which there is a great deal more in the world than either the white or the black; but we must also say this of it; that while white is white, it is only a question of degree for grey to shade into black. There is one acid test which can be applied to every variety of operation—in white magic the operation is always designed and carried out with due regard to cosmic law; any operation which takes no account of cosmic law but goes its own way regardless of what the spiritual principles of the matter may be, can be classified as grey; and any operation which deliberately defies cosmic law can be classified as black.

Let us make this clear by examples. Some people, finding the mental diet of modern life deficient in spiritual vitamins, turn to the inspiration of the ancient pagan gods. This is not black magic provided one recognizes that Aphrodite Ana-dyomene is one thing, and Aphrodite Cotytto is another. It is, in fact, a very useful corrective medicine for the modern mind. It is one, moreover, that we take in constant small doses without knowing it, because so much of art and poetry draws its inspiration from the classics. This is an operation which narrow-minded persons might call black magic, but no one with any insight into life or knowledge of psychology would consider it so.

On the other hand, indiscriminate dabbling in seances, fortune-telling, psychism, and suchlike is classified as grey under our definition, because it takes no account of anything save personal desires, and never asks itself what may be the spiritual quality of what it is doing. No obvious evil being immediately forthcoming, and in fact a plentiful amount of specious piousness being very much in evidence—a form of piousness wherein God is called upon to bless what is being done, but is never asked whether it is according to His will—it is taken for granted that what is afoot is a harmless entertainment, or even actively edifying as tending to raise the mind above materialism, thus reinforcing faith; the after-effects are not considered, and experience shows that the after-effects are far-reaching, and though they may not necessarily involve moral deterioration in persons of naturally wholesome character—and we must acquit them of that charge so often brought—they do cause a marked deterioration in the quality of the mind, and especially of the capacity for logic and judgment. Any form of promiscuous psychic or supernormal dabbling is definitely undesirable, in my opinion, and unfits the person who indulges in it for serious work.

CHAPTER IX

A Magical Body

JAMES Branch Cabell has a story of the dull, ordinary Felix Kennaston who makes for himself an imaginary personality named "Horvendile" through whom he experiences high adventure. Such play is common with children, but the shades of the prison house close around most of us, and a field of fascinating experience and experiment is lost just when it is becoming fruitful. In the vicarious imaginings of film and novel we find a substitute for the creations of our own imagination that we are too dull or too self-conscious to trust any longer.

When the girders of the mind are unloosed in psychopathic states, the creative imagination produces strange things for our undoing. It may terrify us with phantasms of the primeval past, or turn us into lotus-eaters neglectful of reality. When the nuclear consciousness retains control, the same destroying element in the psyche can be disciplined into creation through art-forms, so sophisticated and stylised that their original content is hardly discernible save when it is working on the traditional material of myth and folklore. Through this connecting link we can trace the relationship between the creative imagination of the artist and the technique of the adept who uses myths as his formulae. Both are working with the same level of the subliminal mind, and each has something of the other in him; perhaps the degree of creativeness in either branch of art or magic depends on the proportion in which the other is present.

There is a technique in the repertoire of the adept by means of which he builds himself just such a vehicle of experience as Cabell made his dreary hero create in the imaginary personality of "Horvendile". Equipped with such an instrument formed out of such stuff as dreams are made on we can enter the dream world of the astral plane and act out therein a dramatic representation of our subliminal lives. Whether this be good for mental health or not depends upon the degree of good sense we bring to it. The escape from reality into fantasy may be a dangerous psychological device, but a holiday from reality may have much to recommend it in the shape of compensation and refreshment.

But if the inner planes be indeed the planes of causation for this world of form and matter, the results of such expeditions may be far-reaching, for we may set in motion all manner of subtle influences whose effects will ultimately reach our bourne of time and space in ever-widening circles. Such enterprises are not to be despised, and patient and bold experimentation may yield results well worth the effort and risk—if risk there be. Personally, I think there is little or none for the well-integrated personality that understands the psychology of the proceeding; no more risk, in fact, than is attached to any other work of the creative imagination to which one trusts oneself—the house may fall upon the bad architect, or the bridge collapse under the incompetent engineer, or any other work of human genius blow up and slay its maker if it be in its nature to explode, but we do not for that reason abandon the work of mechanical invention as too risky to be a justifiable field of human endeavour.

So here are some notes on the subject of such experiments, tentative, for the work is in its early stages, but useful perhaps as throwing light on obscure aspects of the human mind, normal as well as abnormal.

I had long been familiar with the method of going forth by night in the Horvendile body, but was unable to practise it successfully until I was given my "magical name". The magical name, whether given by the teacher or discovered by oneself, seems to be an important point in the process of the formulation of the Horvendile body; it appears to play the same part as the grain of sand plays in the formation of the pearl. The psychology of the uses of the magical name needs more study than I can give it at the moment without digression. It must suffice to say that its uses are traditional and I have proved its efficacy in practice. Like most people of vivid imagination I am no stranger to the indulgence in flights of fancy wherein I am the centre of romantic adventures in my own person; like most fiction writers I have put something of myself into my characters; but the creation of a magical personality is a different matter, for if it is to be of any value, it must be in every way greater than oneself, and how can the part be more than the whole that gives rise to it?

The problem is apparently solved by going back into the past of our evolutionary history to a period when the intellect had not obliterated the primitive levels of consciousness, and using the mind of to-day to direct the sublimal activities. It is, in fact, the method of the psychopath reversed, for in his case it is the primitive levels that rise up and flood the conscious mind, usurping the throne of the nucleus of consciousness.

It may be that the use of the magical name has some relationship to the process of going back into time past and reawakening the mode of consciousness of a phase of development long outgrown. Primitive names are imitative sounds or descriptive phrases, and so the barbarous syllables of the magical names may serve to awaken memories in the far-wandering soul. We cannot unfold in evolution that which was not infolded in involution; we forget that a phase of preparation must precede all manifestation. We possessed powers in the primitive phases of our development which have had to be sacrificed in order to achieve the higher powers of the human mind. If, while retaining these powers, we can recover the lost secrets, we have the means of fashioning a Horvendile consciousness that shall transcend the limits of its creator, for we have added the past to the present, or, if another terminology be preferred, we have extended consciousness into the realms usually occupied by subconsciousness.

In my own experience of the operation, the utterance to myself of my magical name led to the picturing of myself in an idealized form, not differing in type, but upon an altogether grander scale, superhuman, in fact, but recognizable as myself, as a statue more than life-size may yet be a good likeness. Once perceived, I could re-picture this idealized version of my body and personality at will, but I could not identify myself with it *unless I uttered my magical name.* Upon my affirming it as my own, identification was immediate. Consciousness transferred itself to the form thus visualized, and I stepped forth into the world of dreams *naked.* Upon that nudity, as of an antique statue, I could, by a simple act of the imagination, put on whatever robes or drapery I desired to symbolize the part I wished to play.

The subconscious level of the mind was built up while humanity was upon the astral plane while coming down the involutionary arc into immersion in matter, and the subconscious mind still retains its astral methods of mentation, which are in terms of emotional values and pictorial images; and it is by obtaining an understanding of the workings of the subconscious mind that we can best appreciate the workings of the elemental consciousness. Equally, it is by recovering access to the subconscious levels of the mind that we become able to function upon the astral plane. It is for this reason that impressions of the astral realms are always greatly confused by the admixture of subjective subconscious elements. The average human subconscious mind in civilized communities is mainly subjective, but the average human subconscious in primitive races is largely objective as well, that is to say, it is conscious of its astral environment; hence the prevalence of magic among primitive peoples, for they are natural magicians. The occultist, in the course of his training, learns to extend the threshold of consciousness once more into the subconscious mind; but whereas in primitive humanity the mentality ended with subconsciousness, in the evolved man, the powers of the human mind return back up the planes and take over the operation of the subconscious astral faculties.

Initiation into the astral plane means more, however, than the exploitation of the psychic powers. The astral plane is the plane of control for the great reservoir of etheric energy, and when we obtain the right of entry upon the astral plane, we also obtain access to and control of the etheric sub-planes of the physical plane. It is from these sub-planes that the vital forces of physical organisms are derived, and it is contact with these great natural reservoirs of force which gives the peculiar magnetic quality so noticeable in souls who have the elemental contacts.

The contacts of the Green Ray are also spoken of as the Celtic Initiation, and for this reason the initiations which were worked by the Greeks and the Druids were of the Upper Astral, in contradistinction to the initiations of an earlier epoch, which were initiations of the Lower Astral, as witness the terrible deities of Akkad and Babylon. The Greeks with their art and the Celts with their music and dance were the true initiates of the Green Ray, and the influence of the astral contacts can be clearly seen to this day in the temperament of the Celtic races.

The Green Ray is essentially the ray of the artist, for it is the subconscious, or astral mind which is the creative factor in the arts, and according to the proportion of this mentation which prevails is the degree of inspiration. Technique is of the conscious human mind, but the true creative artistic impulse is of the ancient astral mind of the race which lies hidden below the threshold of superimposed consciousness. Without the technique so painfully acquired by the discipline of hand and eye, there can be no manifestation in matter of the creative astral impulse. There are many such, who, having the astral contacts cannot reduce them to the forms of the physical plane. These tend to get drawn off that plane and over into the astral, and we see in them those extremes of the artistic temperament which tend towards mental unbalance.

Equally, there are certain types of insanity, and certain symptoms in several insanities of purely physical origin, which can be explained in the light of our knowledge of the astral realm, for just as there are certain drugs of the hashish variety which artificially open the psychic centres to the perception of the astral, so there are certain toxic conditions of the blood which act in the same way, and this explains many of the hallucinations of the insane, who are really experiencing a pathological psychism, and seeing about them the denizens of the astral, and also their own thought-forms with which their own auras teem. Psychology explains the latter phenomena quite satisfactorily, but it does not understand the former, and has recourse to far-fetched explanations in order to bring it into line with the previous class of phenomena which it is able to account for satisfactorily. The psychology of insanity is able to throw light upon many of the phenomena of psychic experience, and this is said in no derogatory spirit, but because it is the simple truth, for the hallucinations of insanity are a type of astral phenomena which have been worked out in the light of modern science.

Many other aspects await that process for their elucidation; and when science, and especially the sciences that deal with the human personality, both mental and physical, realize the function and nature of the astral influences working in and upon dense matter, a great step will have been taken and a new era of scientific discovery opened up. At the present moment we are hovering upon the eve of this realization, as a drop of water hangs on the lip of a beaker; when the force of gravity overcomes capillary attraction, the flow will commence. When there is a realization of the invisible, imponderable realities, a new era of scientific discovery and therapeutic achievement will open up. It is a lack of this realization which is baffling science at the present moment and rendering abortive such lines of research as the investigation of cancer and the endocrines, both, as the occultist knows, so intimately connected with the astral plane.

We may well ask why any serious student of occultism, (and none others are wanted in the Mysteries), should seek the contacts of the Green Ray in the present age, when both the Hermetic and Christian contacts are open to him. The Hermetic student seeks them in order to complete his intiations, so that he may be able to bring the powers down the planes to their final manifestation on the physical plane. Especially is this contact necessary to him if he be also an esoteric therapeutist, for the processes of both disease and repair are intimately associated with astral conditions, which influence consciousness directly and the physical body indirectly through their effect upon the etheric double. The esoteric therapeutist must therefore of necessity have the contacts of the astral plane.

CHAPTER X

The Occult Field Today

THE publication of two very important books on magic, *The Tree of Life* by Israel Regardie, and *Magick* by the "Master Therion" (Aleister Crowley), makes it advisable for the Fraternity of the Inner Light to define its position in these matters. It will be obvious to anyone who compares these books with each other and with the method that is explained in my book *The Mystical Qabalah* that the same system is being used in all three. Some explanation is therefore desirable lest anyone be accused of plagiarism, or stealing another person's thunder; or, equally, be regarded as associated with, or representative of, one of the others.

The explanation is quite simple: all three are drawing from the same source, which I have always referred to as the Western Esoteric Tradition. This Tradition was reorganized and made available for English students by the late S. L. MacGregor Mathers, into whose hands came a number of cipher MSS., and who had the occult knowledge necessary for their use. He claimed to have got into touch with the sources whence these MSS. emanated, and there is a certain amount of objective evidence in support of this claim; but the whole subject is wrapt in mystery by the extreme secrecy he observed, and by the drastic initiation oaths demanded of all to whom he taught what he had learnt; and even to these he was extremely uncommunicative on many vital points.

But be that as it may; and whether he came by his system as he said he did, or whether he made it up out of his own head, in actual practice it worked as a highly efficient and satisfactory system of practical occultism and a Way of Initiation. The proof of the pudding is in the eating in occult affairs; high-sounding titles and limitless claims, such as certain American organizations have accustomed us to in these matters, carry no weight at all with those who have any knowledge of the subject and its history or any practical experience of its workings. It is one of the points in favour of the genuineness of MacGregor Mathers' claims that he wrapped himself in the most impenetrable secrecy and could not be tempted out from his shell even in self-defence.

The evidence concerning the sources from which Mac-Gregor Mathers obtained his MSS. is, so far as I have been able to sift it, inconclusive and conflicting, and a good deal has been said about those MSS. which cannot be substantiated. But that those MSS. exist I can vouch for as a fact, because I know reliable people who have actually seen them; but as they were in cipher, my informants were not much the wiser, nor could they say how much Mac-Gregor Mathers got out of them, and how much he added on as original work.

To get accurate information on the subject was not easy, especially as I came on the scene late in the day, after MacGregor Mathers' death, and it was rather like trying to obtain evidence concerning the nature of the cloth from which were made the robes of the King with No Clothes On. Everybody pledged their immortal souls as to the truth of the legends that were current in the Order that he founded; accepting them uncritically as they circulated by word of mouth and gained authority from much repetition.

So far as I could see, from what I could learn of the matter and what I saw of the people concerned, MacGregor Mathers had a wide range of rare but not very accurate or profound knowledge, in which professional scholars were able to pick holes; but in him were the roots of the matter, for he saw the mystical and philosophical significance behind what he had reaped in the queer fields of Alchemy, the Qabalah, and Egyptology. To him came, by the curious concatenation of invisible forces that are called chance, the famous cipher MSS., and in them he found the formulae which formed the basis of his rituals. These gave him the keys to the queer mass of crazy metaphysical ironmongery which he had already discovered to be a lock. He inserted the psychic key in the metaphysical lock, and lo! it turned and the door of supernormal consciousness was flung open.

How much of the ceremonies were given verbatim in the cipher MSS., and how much was contrived by Mathers out of his knowledge with the aid of the keys with which the MSS. supplied him, I do not know; but I am quite satisfied, from my experience of them, that the system he worked contained factors quite out of the ordinary, which were not the fruits of pure scholarship, however recondite. If Mac-Gregor Mathers was the sole original author of that system, then he was one of the world's greatest men; but from what I saw of his Order, I do not think he was that.

The effect of the ceremonies and methods taught by Mac-Gregor Mathers was to produce the most remarkable psychic experiences and extensions of consciousness in those who had any psychic capacity at all; the methods and aim of these processes were intelligently taught in the higher grades in certain sections of this Order, and it was possible for those so instructed to produce the results at will, and the effect of repeated experiments was cumulative. They obtained, in fact, by psychic methods, the same results other people achieved by the use of such drugs as hashish and mescal, and without the disastrous after-effects that result from "loosening the girders of the mind" by physical means.

In the light of the experience thus gained, the ancient Mysteries became comprehensible, and the possibilities of psychic work thus unfolded were simply limitless. Individual students varied enormously in their capacity to employ the means placed at their disposal; some were merely futile; some were dry-as-dust scholars, frightened out of their lives of obtaining any practical results from the formulae, and some became genuine adepts with signs following. Among the latter was Aleister Crowley, who has written upon occultism under his own name and various pseudonyms, among other, the Master Therion, Frater P., Perdurabo, and a varied assortment.

Some ten years before I came in touch with Mathers'

organization there were wars and rumours of wars. The truth of the matter is hard to come by, but when both sides claim to be angels opposed by devils, it is probably a case of six of one and half a dozen of the other. Anyway, as a result of the quarrel, Crowley published the bulk of Mac-Gregor Mathers' secrets in his magazine, *The Equinox*, and Mathers cursed Crowley with bell, book and candle.

The Order suffered severely during the first World War, and Mathers himself died in Paris from influenza during the epidemic. When I came in touch with his organization, it was manned mainly by widows and grey-bearded ancients, and did not appear to be a very promising field of occult endeavour.

But I had had considerable experience of practical occultism before I made its acquaintance, and I immediately recognized power of a degree and kind I had never met before, and had not the slightest doubt but that I was on the trail of the genuine tradition, despite its inadequate exposition. For some reason best known to themselves, the elucidations and interpretations had been withdrawn into the innermost Inner by the secret chiefs, who simply sat upon them like broody hens on china eggs. The organization had broken up into a number of *disjecta membra*, and everybody regarded everybody else with suspicion as not being of the true orthodoxy.

I, for my part, took no part in the human pettinesses of the mundane plane, but worked at the system, and the system yielded fruits. Other people, I think, must have done the same, among them, Mr Regardie. At any rate, in his two books, *The Garden of Pomegranates* and *The Tree of Life*, he teaches the Golden Dawn system as I learnt it in the various branches of the Order of which I have been a member.

Mr Regardie acknowledges his indebtedness to Mac-Gregor Mathers and Wynn Westcott, but he only quotes from their published works. He quotes so extensively from Crowley, especially from his four-volume work, *Magick*, in which is reprinted the best of the *Equinox* articles and some additional material, and his viewpoint so exactly expresses the best aspects of Crowley's teaching, that I conclude that Crowley's Order, the A.A., not Mather's G.D., is his source. The A.A., however, drew its magical system from the G.D., therefore for all practical purposes Regardie is using the Mathers' system, just as I am myself.

Regardie's two books I unhesitatingly recommend; *The Tree of Life* in particular is a magnificent piece of work, in my opinion the best book on magic that has ever been published. Crowley's *Magick*, of which Regardie makes much use and to which he acknowledges his indebtedness, is also very valuable to the student, but only the advanced student could use it with profit. It is very uneven in its literary quality; contains much grossness and ribaldry, like all Crowley's writings, and much of it is deliberately obscure and allusive. The formulae, too, on which he works, would be considered averse and evil by occultists accustomed to the Qabalistic tradition, for he uses 11 instead of 10 as the basis of his batteries of knocks in the magical ceremonies, and 11 is the number of the Qliphoth, or Evil Sephiroth; a battery of 11, therefore, is an invocation of the Qliphoth. No hint is given of this in the text, and it is an ugly trap for the unwary student.

Crowley also gives the North as the holy point towards which the operator turns to invoke, instead of the East, "whence light arises", as is the classical practice. Now the north is called "the place of greatest symbolic darkness", and is only the holy point of one sect, the Yezidees, or devil worshippers. It is obvious, therefore, that the student who is rash enough to experiment with a battery of 11 knocks and an invocation to the north, is not going to contact what most people would consider to be desirable forces.

Crowley has, however, a remarkable insight into the philosophy of occultism, and when he expounds this, he is a most illuminating writer, and I, for one, would not wish to minimize my debt to his writings; his practical methods, however, are another matter, and are, in my opinion, too dangerous to meddle with in any shape or form.

If I read the signs aright, MacGregor Mathers, Crowley, Regardie and myself are all working on the same formula, the formula contained in the mysterious cipher MSS, discovered by Mathers; Regardie draws from Mathers via Crowley; I imagine, however, that he is alive to the alterations in the formulae that Crowley introduced, for they do not appear in his books, and the formulae he gives are the ones familiar to me in the Golden Dawn workings. These I have found to be sound and effectual; Crowley's version of them I consider to be averse and destructive, though I cannot speak from personal experience on the subject, as I have never had any dealings with his method. I have talked with a number of people who have, however, and there seem to be no two opinions on this point after a sufficient time has elapsed to allow end-results to be seen.

But while I entirely dissociate myself from Crowley's methods, I would not wish to minimize his contribution to occult literature, which is of the highest value. From his books the advanced student, who knows how to read between the lines and refine the gold from the dross, can learn an immense amount, and if our interest is limited to an author's writings, we need not concern ourselves with his personal character or private life.

One of the most difficult problems in occultism today concerns the question of authority. What constitutes a genuine initiation? In what does a genuine occult Order consist? Who and where are the Masters? We need to answer all these questions unequivocally and to define standards of judgment before we can put one foot before another on the Path. I do not propose in these pages to discuss these questions in detail, for I have done so elsewhere, but I shall make a definite attempt to define a standard of judgment in occult matters that shall enable an opinion to be formed in specific cases.

Authority which is wrapt in mystery is a thing that is singularly liable to abuse, and it is very difficult to see how, in the absence of persecution, it can have any justification. When occultism had to be pursued at the risk of life and liberty it was a different matter, but why in the name of common sense should any occult organization burrow underground at the present day? Individuals may find it wise to conceal their interest for professional or social reasons, but it is difficult to see why any professed occult teacher should make a secret of his doings save for the reason that human nature loves a mystery and a modicum of theatricality enhances his prestige. But the dedicated initiator, and none other is worthy of consideration, looks upon esoteric science as a philosophy and a religion, and has no use for such banalities, leaving them to the quack, who finds in mystery-mongering an effectual form of publicity.

We may take a sponge, then, and wipe clean off the slate any individual or organization which cannot or will not put the cards on the table and reveal its antecedents.

It is an unfortunate thing that popular taste has been fed on occult marvels to such an extent that the wholesome fare of actual fact has become repugnant to it. Unless the spiritual ancestry of an order or an initiator is remote both in time and space, there is no prestige. The charlatan takes advantage of this, and reaps the harvest of claims which it is as impossible for us to examine as it is for him to substantiate. Whatever it may be in the East, the lines of contact on the physical plane in the West have been so utterly broken and destroyed within historical time that they have to be pieced together like ancient pottery, Experience proves, however, that when a certain amount of piecing has been done and the pattern appears, it is possible for the psychic to pick up the inner plane contacts and reforge the link. This is what is actually done in the modern Mysteries.

Because an initiator or an organization claims descent from the Himalayan Brotherhood or the Rosicrucians, or any other of the much-advertised secret Orders, it does not follow that that descent is by an unbroken line of tradition on the physical plane; neither does it follow, even if there is no such line of descent, that the claim is invalid. It is possible for an occultist of a certain degree of development to pick up the psychic contacts of these great inner plane organizations and to be working under their influence. When this occurs, very curious things happen on the physical plane, and the worker finds that he is constantly picking up the broken fragments of the tradition to which he is dedicated.

In my own experience I can see, on looking back, that for at least three years before I came in touch with it on the physical plane, I was working on the contacts of the Order into which I was finally received. These contacts I also picked up at different points on the two occasions when they had been totally severed on the physical plane. One appears to be running on invisible rails when once the contacts of one of the great Fraternities has been picked up. There is a large body of testimony to bear witness to this fact.

An occult Order might be likened to an iceberg, of which one-seventh floats above the surface of the water and the rest is submerged. Six-sevenths of occult work is performed on the inner-planes, and of that, five-sixths consist of subjective experiences. The vital thing, then, for any student or initiator, is to have the inner plane contacts of a valid Order; given these, the outer aspect will begin to crystallize around it in the same way as the pearl is laid down layer by layer round the grain of sand in the oyster's shell.

But although the inner plane contact is the vital nucleus, any student or initiator would be in a poor way if he had no body of mundane knowledge to draw upon. The occult systems are too intricate and too detailed for their psychic discernment to be a practical matter.

A great body of tradition exists, though scattered and concealed, and the student in whom the inner eye is open can penetrate its significance when he studies it. If he aims at being an initiator and training students, it is necessary that he should codify this knowledge and reduce it to an intelligible system; the value of an occult school depends in large measure on the manner in which this purely mundane work has been done. The Ancient Wisdom must be correlated with modern thought if its significance is to be made available for the student.

An occult school, then, needs to contain psychics who have the living contacts and scholars who have the relevant knowledge. Given these two things, ancient charters are of little significance; for unless the living contacts are there, and unless the system has been kept up to date generation by generation, charters may be nothing but gravestones marking the burial-place of a dead faith.

Mystical organizations are not long-lived things; they seldom survive the generation that had personal contact with the founder, As soon as the original impulse loses its momentum, senility sets in, and they have to be re-born amid throes unspeakable. Old bottles will seldom hold new wine, and reform usually takes place by schism rather than by expansion and re-statement.

If we seek the roots of living spiritual experience, we are unwise to look for it along the lines of organized physical plane tradition. The wind bloweth where it listeth, not where it is chartered by established authority. The real line of contact is a personal one, and works in a very peculiar, but very definite way. The connecting thread is of the slenderest, yet nevertheless it is there. It is like the grain of leaven that was worked into seven measures of meal— minute, indispensable and effectual. This indispensable physical plane link appears to consist in a personal meeting between the seeker and someone who possesses the inner plane contacts. In every record of the foundation of an Order we read of a meeting between its founder and an illuminated teacher who gave him his contacts by virtue of his personal magnetism.

Abraham, the father of the spiritual Israel, met that mysterious figure, Melchisedec, who came to him bearing bread and wine for the first Eucharist. Jesus, on the eve of His ministry, sought out John the Baptist, the last of the prophets of Israel. Christian Rosencreutz travelled to Damcar, or Damascus, in search of an initiator. Abramelin found the promised instructor among the hermits of the Egyptian desert. Rudolph Steiner met his teacher in the Black Forest. Mme Blavatsky met a certain Indian Adept in

Kensington Gardens during the Jubilee celebrations. McGregor Mathers found the mysterious cipher manuscripts and communicated with an address contained therein.

But let it be clearly noted that the personal contact with an initiated adept, though the turning-point of each career, was no more than a clue that had to be unravelled. Mme. Blavatsky had to write her books and build up her organization. McGregor Mathers used his unique scholarship to give visible body and form to the system of which he received no more than the keys. In each case the greatness of the work accomplished depended upon the calibre of the worker. There must have been many who contacted the teachers of these great pioneers and no doubt received enlightment according to their capacity, but who built nothing in the way of an organization and have left no mark on the world.

Be it noted also that each of the systems thus founded had wrought into their structure the inherent weaknesses of their founders, and these weaknesses formed the lines of fissure along which they ultimately crumbled. Mme Blavatsky had very little discernment where human character was concerned, and though her devotion to her ideals was unquestioned, she was singularly unwise in her policy and unscrupulous in her methods. The "Back to Blavatsky" movement, in its condemnation of modern Theosophy, would do well to remember that the weeds to which they are putting the sickle are but the full growth of the seed she sowed in her unwisdom and lack of principle. McGregor Mathers too, who had no other source of income than his esoteric school, steadily weakened it and finally broke it up by his suspiciousness and exclusiveness.

From these observed facts we learn several things that are of importance to us in forming our standard of judgment. We learn, firstly, that physical tradition, save in so far as it consists of the written word which can be studied, is not of supreme importance, because the real value of a long line of spiritual lineage is in the group mind on the inner planes, and this can be picked up by psychic contact even by those who are not the heirs of the mundane line of inheritance. Moreover, the legal heirs may most lamentably fail to keep the channels open, and so be blind leaders of the blind. Function, not charter, alone gives the right to work the Mysteries.

Secondly we learn that it is not enough to cry Lord, Lord, loudly and persistently; there must be an adequate equipment of scholarship and organization on the physical plane to enable the spiritual forces to find a channel. It has been truly said that the power of endurance of a faith depends entirely upon its literature. All the great faiths have as their nucleus a book, a Bible, a Koran, or the Upanishads. Whatever spiritual teacher relies upon oral teaching leaves no permanent record behind him. There must be a book, and a mystical or holy book, which speaks, not to reason and intelligence, but to intuition and faith. The specific statements of the Neo-Theosophical literature of the Besant-Leadbeater school, which attempt to enlighten and convince the conscious mind, are not the centre round which the movement founded by Mme Blavatsky is rallying its shattered forces; it is *The Secret Doctrine* which is the sacred book that will hold the movement together long after *The Lives of Alcyone* have been mercifully forgotten.

There must be a book, written under the influence of a powerful spiritual inspiration, which forms the permanent nucleus of any movement that is to survive its founder. Such a book exalts the consciousness of those who read it and puts them in psychic touch with the sources whence the inspiration came; they are then able to work independently. People are never satisfied to be spoon fed indefinitely, and unless a system is able to give them these living contacts, it will fail to hold any but the young souls, and of such a movement cannot be built.

It will be interesting to see whether the mass of Rudolph Steiner's writings will afford such a book for his students. I am inclined to doubt whether they are quite of that calibre. McGregor Mathers left behind him the superb rituals of his

Golden Dawn, and these, with their mass of symbolism and magical effectualness, form an inexhaustible mine of inspiration to the initiates of his tradition, which in consequence rekindles its fires whenever there are eyes to see.

We have an inspirational nucleus in the *Cosmic Doctrine*. We also connect up with the Golden Dawn contacts. It has been our endeavour from the first to make our system self-acting and independent of personal teaching. At the present moment it is somewhat like an arterial road in course of construction—there are long stretches of broad highway, and there are bottle-necks and narrow bridges where construction work is going on. We believe, however, that we have the necessary nucleus of permanency in our system, and that it will survive the generation that saw its beginning, and permit of the expansion necessary to adapt it to the needs of future generations, because it depends on method rather than on doctrine.

SUBVERSIVE ELEMENTS IN THE OCCULT MOVEMENT

The occult movement has always been an object of suspicion to the powers that be, and not unreasonably so, for the secrecy in which it tries to shroud itself naturally attracts more attention than it avoids; moreover, this very system of secrecy can conveniently be used as a cloak for other things than occultism, and has so been used on many occasions in the past. The occultist, therefore, cannot reasonably resent the suspicion he has aroused, but should endeavour, by all the means available to him, to clarify the situation, give proof of his *bona fides*, and so conduct his affairs that they shall not afford a cover to evil-doers.

The influences at work in the world today range themselves under two banners, as they have always done. The choice of a banner is a matter of temperament; it has been truly said that everyone is a Radical in his youth and a Die-hard in his old age. We shall always find that the timid, and those whom the god of this world has blessed, are on the side of conservatism, or the maintenance of the present state of affairs. We shall also find that the bolder spirits, and those upon whom the prevailing social system presses hardly, desire to bring about changes in the order of things, and sometimes radical changes. In both camps we shall find moderate men and extremists; this is also a matter of temperament.

These two contrasting types of temperament have difficulty in understanding each other's view-point, and the more extreme examples usually lack the imagination to be able to conceive that there can be a reasonable view-point other than their own; consequently relations tend to become acrimonious, and each party endows the other with vices it does not possess, or is run by only a small and unrepresentative minority. Self-interest also exacerbates the situation, for any gains on the part of one party can only be at the expense of losses to the other. The two camps tend to become armed camps, with a perpetual guerilla warfare going on between them that occasionally develops into a campaign on a vast scale.

Within limits, both aspects are essential to the well-being of the body politic; so clearly has experience proved this, that a well organized Opposition is considered essential to the transaction of national business.

But although the normal polarity of view-point is a wholesome check on extremes of any kind, and a normal and inevitable development in this universe which manifests through pairs of opposites, there are to be found in both camps extreme view-points which pass all bounds of equilibrium, and, to use again the language of the Qabalists, are Qliphothic, because they tend towards Chaos. The Die-hard would retain vested interests in his dead hand, regardless of changing conditions or the welfare of the world as a whole; and the anarchist, in his disgust with existing conditions, would destroy them from the foundations upward, thus bringing down the house of life on his own head and leaving himself without shelter while the rebuilding is in progress. Reasonable men of both parties regard their own extremists with distrust and are able to give both sympathy and respect to their opponents.

As we have already noted, the choice of a party is usually dictated by temperament rather than intellectual conviction. Those who are to be found in the party of change are usually of a more imaginative and impressionable temperament than those who find their spiritual home in conservatism, using the word in its dictionary and not its political sense. It is the same type of person who has an open ear for all things new in any department of the world's activities; he is generally unconventional in dress and diet; wears his hair long when other people wear it short, as in modern times; and short when other people were wearing it long, as among the Roundheads; and reacts violently to his own complexes in general, not only in the things of his especial conviction, but in all his way of life, whether in petty social usages or in the deeper and more fundamental things of the spirit.

Occultism being, more than most things, an unconventional view-point, we find among its adherents a high percentage of the liberal-minded, and comparatively few of those with a conservative or conventional outlook. We must not, however, commit the logical fallacy of confusing *post hoc* with *propter hoc*. People do not become radical in their views because of any doctrines taught them under the veil of secrecy in occult lodges, but become occultists because they are of the open-minded and adventurous type.

There is, moreover, a certain type of the more philosophic reformer who, in seeking an explanation which shall direct him to the root-causes of social discontent, finds that the esoteric teachings afford that explanation, especially in their doctrines concerning group minds, subtle influences and evolutionary cycles. Such a social reformer studies occultism, not for the purpose of applying ritual magic to his enemies, as popular imagination supposes, but in order to understand root-causes.

It is rare to find the fanatic of either party in occult circles, or, for the matter of that, in any circles that do not see eye to eye with him; he has such a one-way mind, and is so concentrated on his special prepossession, that he is not interested in anything else, and has no time to waste on it.

It will be seen, then, that although people with advanced and unconventional view-points unquestionable predominate in occult circles, they do so incidentally and temperamentally, and not because the occult doctrines are immediately concerned with politics.

OCCULTISM AND THE UNDERWORLD

Apart from what might be termed the genuine and sincere association of occultism with subversive persons and ideas, which is purely accidental, depending upon the fact that the same type of temperament takes to both lines of interest, it cannot be denied that, inextricably mixed in with the occult movement is a dangerous underground line of subversive activity, and the authorities do well to keep a watch upon it. The peculiar, and quite needless, secrecy observed by occultists makes the occult movement a very handy cloak for various activities that will not bear inspection.

Scotland Yard is quite alive to this fact, and keeps a sharp eye on all occult organizations in consequence. The semi-public, semi-private nature of the proceedings lending themselves singularly well to the purposes of persons whose activities are under surveillance in their customary haunts. Any esoteric organization which is asked to allow letters to be sent in its care, or to receive parcels from printers to be called for by private car, or even to allow its telephone to be used by strangers, ought to be on its guard. It is an open secret that the letters of suspects are examined, and that their telephone calls are listened to; consequently it is of great importance to such persons to find unsuspected places where they can receive communications. There can very seldom be a good reason for having letters sent to an accommodation address, and esoteric organizations which are complacent in this matter make difficulties for the whole movement.

It is a very unfortunate thing that the Theosophical Society became so intimately associated with Indian political activities, though in justice it must be said that there was probably no realization of what extremes these activities would ultimately lead to. Many people in consequence look upon all occult movements as being tarred with the same brush, and fear that they will be involved in all manner of complications if they become associated with them, and therefore limit their studies to the theory of esoteric science and find no opportunity for experience of its practice.

The Fascistically-inclined organizations of Great Britain seem to take the menace of subversive occultism very seriously, and to consider that an occult society is, *ipso facto*, subversive, and as such to be spied upon. No reasonable person should object to being inspected by the authorized representatives of law and order, because his own interests are protected in the so doing; but the amateur detective is an offensive nuisance, and as such, must expect just as short shrift as the Bolshevik.

The part played by drug addiction in the seamy side of occultism has been greatly over-rated. The drugs used are of the vision-producing type, such as anhalonium and hashish, and these are not drugs of addiction in the West. In the quantities in which they are used for occult experiments they are unlikely to do permanent harm.

The drugs to which people become addicts are those which either produce exhilaration and immunity to fatigue, or those which deaden consciousness and make a troubled life more bearable; under neither of these headings are to be found any of the vision-producing drugs. No one is likely to induce vision by their use sufficiently frequently to run any risk of addiction; and in any case, anhalonium is not habit-forming.

The risk to which these drugs expose those who use them is psychic, not physical; they may, if the experimenter is not an expert occultist, thoroughly competent in sealings and banishings, lay their user open to psychic invasion, and even obsession, because they open the doors of the astral to the unprepared consciousness, and as every swimmer knows, it is one thing to swim out, and another to swim back. I am not prepared to deny that they have a place in occult research, but such research should only be undertaken by those who are properly equipped, both as to their occult and their scientific attainments, and is in every way undesirable when done by those who are merely seeking a new thrill.

A great deal has been made by fiction writers of the Black Mass, which consists of desecrating by every means that an overwrought imagination can suggest, the sacred symbols of the Catholic faith. It is a procedure limited for all practical purposes to Roman Catholics, because, as Eliphas Levi pointed out, no one can partake of a Black Mass effectually who does not fervently believe in a White Mass. To the Nonconformist, the operations of a Black Mass would be senseless.

Sexual orgies have played a part in the Mysteries, and in the case of primitive peoples, we must not be too ready to condemn indiscriminately without considering the type of society in which they take place. Civilized standards cannot be used to judge primitive folk living under entirely different conditions and codes to ourselves. These orgies by no means necessarily produce the degeneration that missionaries would have us believe. They are by no manner of means the same thing as general sexual promiscuity, but are strictly limited to certain periods. A people living under natural conditions, in the most intimate touch with nature, and competing with plant and animal for the possession of the soil, has other social needs, and consequently other moral standards, than a highly organized, dense population, whose problem is to feed itself from a limited area. To the former, the orgies that stimulate fecundity may be as necessary and virtuous as the moral restraints of other types of society.

Nor must we make the mistake of thinking that because a race has either explicit or symbolic representations of the organs of reproduction among its sacred symbols it is necessarily licentious, any more than the fact that a nun is admitted to a religious Order with a marriage ceremony should lead us to suspect the same thing. Reticence in sexual questions is a matter of manners, not of morals.

There are truths in these things that we cannot ignore, and civilization is the poorer, and by no means either the cleaner or the healthier, for ignoring them. The trouble comes, however, when people who are licentiously inclined use them as a justification and a cloak. A certain amount of this has been done, especially on the Continent, in the name of occultism. For the most part, however, the loose living in occult circles consists in a somewhat freely circulating assortment of "soul-mates", and has no more occult significance than similar conditions in artistic cricles. No magical use is made of the relationships; the only occult touch they have lies in the finding of justification for them in past lives, which no one except the persons concerned takes very seriously.

Various occultists, at different times, have attempted to put into practice the Freudian doctrines. No one with any insight into life can deny that there is a very large measure of truth in these doctrines, and that theoretically much justification can be found for the doings of such initiators. The social consequences, and the general strain and upheaval of such methods are, however, so serious that, whatever one may think of them from the point of view of pure science, in actual practice they are better left alone. For one thing, the forces employed get out of hand extremely easily, and when such practices are done in group formation, the group-mind takes on an atmosphere much too elemental to be tolerated by civilized people. Orgies and crude sexual magic have passed away from the level of consciousness at which civilized races function, just as infanticide and the despatch of the aged have passed away.

There are other, and better, methods of approaching the elemental levels of consciousness than these which do not belong to the Right Hand Path. By purely psychological methods the psycho-analyst achieves the same result; but it is only when the experience of the psycho-analyst is united to the knowledge of the esotericist that the deeper issues and supremest heights are reached.

At one time there was a widespread use of abnormal vice for magical purposes; the facts are well known and gave rise to repeated scandals. There is nothing to be said in mitigation of such practices; they are unnatural and destructive on every plane. There is reason to believe, however, that this phase of Black Occultism has had its day and is dying out. The principal exponent became hopelessly insane, and his example appears to have taught wisdom to such of his followers as had not learnt it from experience. Nevertheless, there remains a great deal of very unsound teaching and practice in certain circles, which produces a rich crop of psycho-pathologies. Group-minds have become tainted, and sensitive individuals are liable to very unpleasant experiences, to much psychic disturbance, and even to actual illness through association with them. The leaders of these groups are by no means given over to evil, but they have very little understanding of the forces with which they have been contacted. The repeated outbreaks of psychic trouble in their midst they attribute to occult attack from outside, or to the retaliation of the forces of evil against which they are contending, and do not realize that they are like people who have built their houses on the slopes of a volcano. However, it is probable that, with the breakdown of the leader, the atmosphere will gradually clear, and that which is of value will be disencumbered of the many unfortunate elements that have gathered about it.

THE "JEWISH PERIL"

There has always been a strong anti-Semite feeling among the continental nations, though in these islands it is of a very modified type. There have been books published recently which have set out to show that the revolution in Russia is the work of the Jews, and that the Jewish race, as an organized unit, is out to destroy civilization. Among these books are some which attempt to prove specifically that the Jewish initiate is a particularly dangerous person, and that any occult movement in which a goodly proportion of Jews finds a place must be a particularly dangerous movement.

In order to examine the rights and wrongs of this proposition we must first examine the basis on which it rests. What is the cause of the general antagonism to the Jew? Most people would say it was because they slew Our Lord, but the real answer to this question is probably to be found in the fact that there is a higher percentage of intellectual acuteness and ability, and a lower percentage of the martial virtues among the Jewish people than among most other races. This together with his racial pride and exclusiveness, irritates the Gentile; and as the Jew is seldom a war-like person, the irritation can safely be given free vent. Moreover, owing to his peculiar gift for finance, the Jew is the universal money-lender; and a very convenient way of putting paid to inconvenient debts is to have an occasional pogrom. Both parties possess strengths and weaknesses which make them feared by, and yet a prey to, each other; such a state of affairs cannot be productive of mutual trust and good feeling.

It is perfectly true that in Bolshevism, and for the matter of that, in anarchical circles in general, there is a high percentage of Jews. The reason for this is not far to seek. The Jew is an exception to the general rule that an idealist is never practical. When an idealistic movement wants an efficient organizer, it generally fails to find it among the Gentiles in its ranks. The Jews have been the backbone of the Bolshevist movement for the simple reason that the Russian, left to himself, cannot organize and is hopelessly impractical, therefore the Jewish element has come to the front. This is not peculiar to the Bolshevist movement. Peter the Great, when reforming the Russian administration and founding the state upon modern lines, found it necessary to import German administrators for the simple reason that then, as now, the Russians could not organize or administer.

The Jew comes to the front in revolutionary circles, as he does in literary and scientific circles, owing to the high percentage of ability and driving-power to be found in his race. Again, *post hoc* is not *propter hoc*.

The Jew is attracted to the Western Esoteric Tradition because it is based on the Qabalah, the mystical wisdom of Israel, and because his intellect is of a type which takes kindly to esoteric philosophy. There appears to be a complete lack of the mystical element in Judaism to-day, save in relation to Jewish nationalism. For women, indeed, this is especially marked, for they have no place in the Jewish religion save as the carriers out of the Levitical customs that apply to the home. This lack seems to be keenly felt by the more thoughtful Jew, who feels the need of the kind of mysticism that Christianity teaches but cannot accept the Christ. He, and especially she, find this mysticism in occultism without any exclusive religious bias, and are able to adapt it to that which they honour in the tradition of Israel. Consequently there are many Jews in Western occultism, and, as always, they come to the front because of their intellectual capacity and driving-force.

It cannot but be obvious to anyone who looks at the matter in the light of history and racial psychology, that the Jewish race, as a race, has more to lose than any other by social upheaval and disorder, for they are the money-lenders of the world, and the first thing any nation does after a revolution is to wipe out back debts, both private and national. The Jewish race are, moreover, non-military; not that there are not individual fighting-men among the Jews, as the history of pugilism shows, but their peculiar religious tenets as applied to social customs make an army very difficult, if not impossible to organize. Upon one occasion Jerusalem was stormed because the Jews would not work at its defences on the Sabbath.

There is no question, however, but that men of Jewish race have played an important part in determining the course of history by giving or withholding the sinews of war from bellicose monarchs and governments. This, however, has not been a matter of organized national policy, but of personal speculation and venture, at any rate since governments have ceased to force the Jew to lend money upon the security of his own back teeth. It is noteworthy that the record of the Jewish statesman is singularly clean; he serves the nation of his adoption with a single-minded integrity and conspicuous ability.

The Jew has always been prominent in Western occultism; in fact he was for centuries its only guardian, for the Church put down all speculation and experiment in spiritual things with a firm hand. The Qabalah has been the chief outlet for the spiritually-minded Jew who found phylacteries barren things; and the Qabalah has ceremonial magic and a highly technical psychism as its practical applications. In Israel is to be found the fountainhead of the Western Tradition; in fact Western occultists need to have a working knowledge of the elements of the Hebrew language in order to disentangle the barbarous jargon of dog-Hebrew which is the heritage of unscholarly lodges.

The fanatic, who has got it firmly fixed in his head that the Jewish race is bent upon the destruction of all social order, looks upon it as one of the clearest proofs of the guilt of occultism that a Jewish element and influence is to be found therein. May we remind them, however, that the same may be said of Christianity, which has its cultural roots in Judaism. From the historical point of view, Abraham rather than Peter holds the keys of heaven for the Western world.

Esoteric tradition admits of no exclusiveness; it is the very essence of its spirit that it blasphemes no God that has been hallowed by man's devotion. It sees all religions as the expressions of man's spirit rather than the personal revelation of a jealous God to His chosen people. It suffers from neither superstitious awe nor bigoted fear. When asked to take sides in any acrimonious dispute concerning ultimate rights and wrongs it says, A plague on both your houses! The way of God is the way of the Lightning flash, zigzagging between the Pillars, and the place of equilibrium is in the central point of the Central Pillar.

CHAPTER XI

Esoteric Glossary

TEACHING on esoteric subjects contains so many vaguely defined terms that it is advisable that those studying in our group should know more precisely what we mean when we use certain of the key-words. Indeed, in some of our earlier papers the meaning is not always as clear as it might be as some time elapsed (as usually happens) before the need for these definitions became evident. We do not legislate for other groups but the definitions we give are in line with the principles behind our teaching and have now been shown by experience to be sound; it does not follow, however, that esoteric *publications* in general use the terms in exactly these meanings and, in fact, the same word with slightly varying significances may sometimes be found in the same publication, making it necessary for the serious reader to be wary lest he gain a false impression, if indeed, the authors knew exactly the impression they wished to give.

The words we have in mind are set out below and in some instances information on the subjects is added.

The Logos is used as meaning the Solar Logos, the God of our solar System. The God of the Cosmos we describe as The First Manifest.

The Manus are primarily "ethnological" leaders on the Inner Planes of the great Root-Races. They depicted in themselves some great Idea or Principle which was behind the esoteric mission of their Root-Race. There is more than one type of Manu. The Manu of a Race is also the prototype or the Ideal Man of a Race, and in this connection the syllable "MAN" in certain languages can be of extreme antiquity and significance. The Manus are of the First Three Swarms —Lords of Flame, Form and Mind—but not all of these Lords are Manus; the Manus are indeed of Archangelic type with *a "multiple Ego"*. This is the nearest approximation in words to these great Beings. Their "personalized" forms, however, appeared in "humanized guise".

The Masters are the perfected beings of the human evolution who guide mankind and perform certain other work rather than "enter into their rest"; they are of various types and grades. They do not become "Lords of Humanity" (see Cosmic Doctrine) until they have passed beyond all that is now known as humanity—even as no grade is established until the next is entered upon.

The Divine Spark may be thought of as the "outer" aspect of the Cosmic Atom stamped with the Logoidal Impress. Until a high grade is attained it may be considered for all practical purposes as being the Cosmic Atom—the immortal part of each one of us, rooted in the Great Unmanifest, of the same *essence* as the Logoi, but vastly junior in development etc.

The Individuality or Higher Self[1] is the unit of an evolution, consisting of the bodies of the highest three planes (using a seven plane system) organized around the Divine Spark.

The Lower Self, Personality, or Projection[1] is the unit of an incarnation consisting of the "bodies" of the four lower planes (in a seven plane system). Its experiences are absorbed in essence after physical death by the Higher Self but this alone does not determine the next Projection as the Higher Self has phases of development between incarnations—based largely on pre-incarnatory (or involutionary) experiences which also influence the next Projection.

The Soul is one of the words most frequently used with differing meanings. We use it as signifying the inner aspects of the Personality plus the outer aspects of the Higher Self. It is, in fact, the unit of evolution up to a certain point (beyond Chesed).[2] The Personality aspects of it are (or should be) absorbed in essence by the Higher Self at death and the soul itself conditioned thereby for its next incarnation. (This is capable of much wider exposition). It can be considered

---

[1] The Society of the Inner Light now uses the terms Evolutionary Personality and Incarnationary Personality, respectively.
[2] On *Tree of Life* of the Qabalah.

as the vehicle of evolving man as far as the Abyss on the Tree of Life and its state at death and after has much to do with the next Personality projected by the Higher Self. Certain "pathologies" of an esoteric nature affecting future incarnations are possible from wrong actions and attitudes of mind by it during incarnation and after death.

Root Races can be used for the original Race from which spring the sub-Races. It often refers to the seven great divisions of the Atlantean Race, and these racial prototypes were further developed in the post-diluvian world into the main racial "families" as known exoterically. As a term "Root-Race" can also refer to the four *colour* divisions of mankind, and also to the five stages of human evolution on this globe—i.e. the Hyperborean, the Lemurian, the Atlantean, etc. The colour divisions and stages of human evolution also had Manus for there are many types of Manu. The White Race contains not only the most evolved—the Aryan —but also the Semites who were intended to bring yet another Ideal to the White Race. Thus did the Manu Melchizedek prepare the way for Jesus the Christ and thus did the Idea of a Messiah become grafted on to the Semitic Tradition. (In the background of all this is a connection with the Holy Grail). Behind the secret history of Israel moves the Archetypal Priest of the Atlantean-Semitic Root-Race; and owing to certain Atlantean errors the Jewish section of this Race have brought this Archetype to the West without themselves being fitted to use it, save for small groups. This is the "Curse of the Jews" and dates from long before the birth of Jesus, though had they accepted him much would have been mitigated. Their theocracy should have grown into a World-State, but they would not share with others.

The Manus of certain Root-Races are known traditionally and some are enumerated:—

RAMA was the Manu of the Aryan Race.

MELCHIZEDEK was the Manu of the Chaldean and early Semitic Races in addition to his Atlantean connection.

NARADA was the Manu of the First Atlantean Race.

ASURAMAYA was a Manu of an earlier Lemurian Race which had mingled with the early Atlanteans, and he "lived" in Atlantis in these earliest days. He was the "teacher of the starry wisdom" to the ante-diluvian world even as was Melchizedek to the post-diluvial, and was the first astronomer. In Atlantis he worked with and under Narada. Euclid—who is a Lord of one of the Wisdom aspects of the Western Tradition (see "Esoteric Orders") was not only a great human teacher but also had on the Inner Planes an aspect manifesting a direct "beam" from Asuramaya, (somewhat analogous but less in degree and origin, to the manifesting of the Christ by the Lord Jesus), which was more than an "overshadowing". This subject is too complex for further reference here.

The Semites were meant to be "Priests of the Most High", but only a small section in a later evolution achieved this in a minor way. The Aryans were Magi and Colonizers.

The Archetypes are original patterns or models of a Divine Idea. Such archetypal (or archetypical) patterns are manifested in various ways:—

(1)   Through the Divine or superhuman Instructors of certain races or nations on whose lives are based the dramatized rituals and the initiations of the various Mysteries.

(2)   Through non-human forms belonging to pre-terrestrial and pre-human types of development such as

(a)   the Signs of the Zodiac (in their actual, not anthropomorphized, form)

(b)   macrocosmic symbols related to the microcosm and based upon the Essential Forces of the Universe such as geometric and phallic ideographs of primary importance. These have passed into the human mind and emerge in dream symbolism but they are older than the human mind.

The traditional names of great archetypal figures are often racial memories of (1) i.e. of the Instructors—and belong to the different phases of evolution passed through by their groups; they originated with some shadowy teacher who had in ancient times guided some particular group. They should not be confused with the archetypal force of a Manu who worked upon the collective main "family" of the whole race of which the group was a part. For example, Rama was the great Leader of the Aryan Race but Orpheus, Osiris, Isis, Odin, Merlin etc. were Instructors of certain Aryan groups and ancestral memories of them passed into some of the gods and heroes of those groups. For, though some of the gods are "natural forces" others are memories of prehistoric teachers.

Racial Angels are high beings of the Archangelic or Angelic Hierarchy appointed since the beginning of the world as guardians of certain groups; they might be described as "personalized principles of Archetypal Fire" who worked first with the Manus and then, on the withdrawal of the latter, continued in contact with the world as guardians of these principles and of the forces surrounding their "earthing" (or establishing in Malkuth). Such a being is referred to in the Biblical phrase "the Prince of the Powers of Persia", a great Racial Angel of a former period. Racial Angels guide races to the territory where they shall take root and as long as a nation remains sufficiently strong (in many senses of that word) the Angel is as its Higher Self so to speak. When that nation decays to such an extent that real contact with the Angel is not possible the Angel withdraws to a nation more capable of expressing the inner Principle he represents. Such Angels will incorporate in their "realm" lesser tribal beings of other nations which become deeply integrated—by conquest or otherwise—with the original territory. The subject is very complex but will repay study; conquest on the physical plane does not always triumph over a nation.

Anima and Animus. These psychological terms are well defined in text-books and reference should be made to such books—such reference is especially needed for psychological expressions, many of which are already used widely and inaccurately. All that need be said here is that Jung should be read with great attention since it is probable he knew more than he cared to express plainly. *When* integration with the Higher Self draws near it is possible that "anima" or "animus" may give place to ideal figures of the same sex as the Personality and such figures may even be foreshadowed at a much earlier stage in sensitive people in the *higher* emotional states.

The Shadow—The Dweller on the Threshold.

The "Shadow" of Jungian psychology should not be confused with the "Dweller on the Threshold". The Shadow represents the subconscious material of the present incarnation, of one life only though, naturally, it is affected by previous lives. The "Facing of the Shadow" implies the realization of the reality of the subconscious mind and the acceptance of material often at variance with that of the conscious mind. It occurs, therefore, at a comparatively early stage in the integration process—corresponding on the Tree of Life to the 32nd Path (the Well) and to Yesod.

The "Dweller on the Threshold" as used in our terminology represents the *entire* past of the individual, all that has gone to make him what he is. It is, therefore, the aggregate of *all* his "Shadows". The "Facing of the Dweller on the Threshold" is the confrontation with the entire past and calls for the full acceptance of that past and of all that has gone to make the individual what he now is. It occurs at a late stage in the integration process. On the Tree of Life it would correspond with a Chesedic initiation whose realizations are completed in Daath where "Past becomes Present". The full implication of the "Dweller on the Threshold" is probably not explicitly set out in psychological writings. It should be noted that the integration here referred to is not the minor one (so to speak) of Tiphareth but a much more complete one which is nowhere fully treated of in published material as far as we know.

The "Dweller on the Threshold" may be seen in vision by those who have such experiences and should not be mistaken for an angelic or Elemental figure of the usual type. It is a manifestation of the *aggregate* debt in a personalized form or may arise from an awareness of that debt, the forms varying in accordance with the nature of the debt. This "vision" or "awareness" must be encountered before the really deep integration and more advanced spiritual progress can be made. It is possible that it will absorb the unregenerate side of the Personality (the "renegade" image or aspect), and something approaching this modern teaching was depicted by the Egyptians in their figure of "The Eater of Hearts". Terrible as can be the Dweller on the Threshold to confront it is yet only an "averse" aspect of the Higher Self ("potentially", or "unabsorbed") and can have something Divine in its appearance for it is connected with the suffering of the Higher Self which "becomes sin" to redeem its projections—a consideration which merits deep meditation. In short, the Dweller on the Threshold is the sum-effect of the individual's past lives, his own averse character rising out of him into seemingly independent life.

The Masters (further to previous reference.)

Just as at certain periods the esoteric work and position of individuals in incarnation are assessed so is the work of the Hierarchy assessed in its relation to the Greater Whole. It should be clearly understood that a Master is one whose function relates to the Solar Logoidal evolution and the Masters should be realized for what they are and their type of functional power understood. In order to function fully in the Solar Logoidal evolution much Cosmic growth has to be made—the "Stellar Initiations" in all their gradations must be completed.

Racial Symbols—Animal. The Race-Soul exudes an "influence" based on an aspect of its character and this "influence" can assume an etheric form; it is a kind of "totem". As the Race develops this becomes one of its especial symbols. The symbol of Britain in this respect—

originally of both Celts and Saxons—is a White Horse. The Lion as a symbol is not so early in origin nor so important being of Norman and heraldic derivation. The White Horse is a very ancient symbol and, if considered as a development of the Eo-Hippos has contact with Atlantis. No special posture—such as "rampant" etc.—is prescribed.

Archetypal Forms and Psychology (see also above).

It is possible, for convenience in use, to divide types of Archetypal Forms into: (1) The Macrocosmic Archetypes such as the Gods which are "personalisations" of great macrocosmic forces, (2) The Microcosmic Archetypes dealt with in modern psychology which are personalizations of the macrocosm in the soul of man. The Microcosmic Archetypes—such as the Father, Mother, Magician, Wise Woman etc.—represent the linking of the developing soul with certain "lines of force" in the macrocosm, or, in other words, the bringing of the manhood to God or the Gods. (In this way behind the Masters is the Supernal Force that may be described as "The Great Sacrifice" and which is linked with the Sacrificed God of the Tree of Life.)

In addition to the Archetypes here mentioned there exist what might be called "complementary forms" of various aspects of the Microcosm, such as the Angel, the Daemon, etc., and the distressing type of Magical Body ensouled with Elemental essence variously called the "Dweller on the Threshold", and the "Evil Genius". It is possible for these to represent whole groups or families but detailed discussion of them here would be too long and difficult for a paper like this; the psychological term of "the Renegade Aspect" of the psyche is applicable to them.

The Contrasexual Image. This is a well-known psychological phenomenon; when recognized for what it truly is it can be a special link between the Personality and the Higher Self, being an aspect of the Angel of the Pillar opposite to the physical sex—that is female for the Silver Pillar, male for the Black Pillar. (These Pillars refer to the composite glyph of the Tree of Life and the Pillars—a Qabalistic symbol.)

Notes on the Grail and kindred symbolism

Contacts and power from the Inner Planes are received on the physical plane either through a group or through an individual who passes on to a group his own contacts made on their behalf. The former method was the basis of the Old Testament Grail—the Ark, the latter was the basis of the New Testament Grail—the Cup or Chalice. Both these receptacles have become symbols, as have other forms of such receptacles—the Dish, the Bowl, the Stone. Before these became symbols *they were facts*. The Ark actually held a substance of the Inner Planes which made a direct contact between God and the Group. In Atlantis the Cup or Bowl was the Moon-Bowl (of the *old* Moon and the earliest stages of mankind) in which was a substance in actual contact with the Supernal. These "substances" are Mysteries and, indeed, a version of what in far later days was known as "the Real Presence", and from memories of them have been developed the sacramental rites of various creeds. The finding of the Cup which had been withdrawn from man because of his sins is behind the Grail legend in which the Cup of the *actual contact* with the Innermost rather than the Cup as a symbol of that contact appeared to certain persons. There are endless possibilities in meditation on this theme, but much can be pieced together from what has already been said. We think of Melchizedek bringing back the sacramental symbol to Abraham; that his home was on Venus-Lucifer and that there is an old legend that the Grail was fashioned from an emerald fallen from Lucifer's crown. The Cup, however, was the ancient Atlantean contact with God stored within the "Moon-Bowl"—it did not hold "wine" in the literal sense. The Lord Jesus (a "high-priest after the Order of Melchizedek") re-instituted it (as at their own levels did such saviours as Orpheus, Mithra etc.). Behind all this is the *secret* history of Israel in the background of which moves the Archetypal Priest of the Semitic Atlantean Root-Race.

Sundry Notes on Astrology

1. The Zodiac comes under the influence of the (12) Cosmic Rays, and the true Zodiacal influence upon the human being dates not from that operating at the moment of the birth-date of his present incarnation but from the Cosmic "groupings" in action at the time when the Divine Spark coming down the planes (see "Cosmic Doctrine") was impressed with some special Zodiacal force. This force, if truly discerned, would be apparent in the astrological positions of each incarnation—also it would be possible to make of the individual influences at work on the Spirit a calculation somewhat analogous to that of the Precession of the Equinoxes at work on the Sun; the subject is difficult and calls for expert and specialized knowledge. Each Divine Spark is respectively influenced by one of the twelve great "Concepts of Truth" which are behind the twelve Great Rays. This is the real fundamental astrology which covers an evolution. The working of the Lesser Zodiac during one incarnation is trivial by comparison, though its understanding can be very helpful.

2. The Zodiac is not so much an imaginary belt as "zones" or "rays" of influence touching the Earth at certain seasons. It is best considered in sets of four constellations. The three modes of force—Cardinal, Fixed, Mutable—refer to the three Rays of Life; there are three sets of these balanced with the Three Rays of Destruction. Each Zodiacal mode is aligned with one of these Rays of Life. The Rays of Life and the Zodiacal Signs equated with them vary with each evolution: the Four Holy Creatures of the present evolution did not rank as such before this evolution—despite the influences they shed. In the next evolution the four "Mutable" Signs will be "holy". The Signs of the Zodiac are the mystical basis of the Cosmos.

3. The sun's passage through the Zodiac resembles the

"gathering of the limbs of Osiris", that is to say the building into the Individuality of the experiences gained from the various incarnations. These may be considered in one way as "types of evolution" on the Path. Arthur's knights, the Twelve Apostles, and similar groupings may be thought of as allegorical figures in this way as well as historical facts in some instances.

If we regard the Sun-power in the horoscope as having the four aspects of horizon, zenith, sunset, and nadir, and as acting through not only the solar Sign itself and that on the ascendant but also through whatever Sign or Planet is on the cusp of the 10th, 7th, and 4th Houses respectively, we find that this is reflected in the initiate's horoscope by the four great Egyptian aspects—Ra, Osiris, Tum, Khepra. The Sun itself is a reflection of Sirius; Venus eventually is transcended in Sothis (Sirius) the home of Isis.

4. Evolutionary changes are already beginning in the Cosmic spheres. Towards the end of an Evolution (covering a vast expanse of time) form itself begins to alter—as happened at the end of the Atlantean Age. At such a time great Cosmic Beings take over from those previously in charge and the "outer" conditions of earth and man begin to change, largely because of "rays" or "influences" from distant stellar forces coming into operation.

(Higher Self/Lower Self contacting.
Martyrdom, Death for a "Cause".)

The Higher Self contacts the Lower Self in many ways. At first, contacts are rare and for the "once-born" may happen only once or twice in a lifetime, showing as an intuitive awareness before some important event. A martyr is always an initiate in some degree even without any esoteric experience or training: in such a type a very deep conviction may be sent down by the Higher Self which must be acted on at all costs by the Lower Self even if suffering and death result. The Higher Self is not, of course, concerned with what the Lower Self understands as the rights of religion or politics but is occupied with some karmic matter to be adjusted by the Lower Self's death or by some motive arising out of Cosmic Law quite unknown to the Lower Self, veiled behind some doctrine or concept. The martyr may well seal with his blood a cause of which in the Lower Self he is quite unaware.

The Glyph of the Crucifixion (considered from two aspects.)

1.   A most important symbol is that of The World-Soul and its Crucifixion. Our Lord "concreted" or "earthed" this glyph in his type of death. The World-Soul, however, is crucified on the Cross of the Elements, a cross which is continually expanding its arms through evolutionary development and, in material matters, through scientific research. The Elemental Cross has to reach its utmost limits of expansion in the present world and at the same time have each arm in perfect balance with the others. The *macrocosmic* Mother of Sorrows and the Great Teacher on either side of the World-Soul on the Elemental Cross make up this great glyph. *Microcosmically* these are represented by Our Lady and St John on either side of the Cross of Calvary. Thus the "dark aspect" of Binah (Ama) is a standing figure (the "white aspect", Aima, is a seated figure). The hymn "*Stabat Mater Dolorosa*" is very significant for it is in form and force a Binah[1] rite, even to its three-fold rhyming structure.

Sorrow in the *macrocosm* implies realization of the Great Law, but in the *microcosm* it implies non-realization. Nevertheless, the deeper the capacity for feeling sorrow, the deeper is the realization eventually achieved.

2.   The Universe is a Logoidal thought-form and its development is the unfolding, as it were, of a dream of God. Even as with man's dreams the Supernal Dream is "interpreted" through a cypher of conditions analogous with what men call symbols. The cypher of this world is best described as a Figure on a Cross. The Logos is aware of Its creation in a summarized form which gradually unfolds its meaning: Images such as this may be called "Arch-Archetypes". It

[1] See *Tree of Life*.

does not greatly matter what name is given to the World-Symbol. It may be termed "Spirit crucified on Matter", or "Man on the Cross of the Elements", and may be aligned with the historic event near Jerusalem some 2,000 years ago. Such a Symbol is bound eventually to become esoterically connected with each one who achieves in this Evolution. The achievement is *first* made through a Redeemer who brings The Image to Malkuth; it is *finally* made by the individual in an individual sense. On each side of the World-Soul stands a figure—one is of the Virgin-Mother who brings forth in sorrow both to generation and regeneration, the other is the Mind of the World-Soul who watches beside it to give it courage and help and is the symbol of the Guides and Masters. Christian history has taken Our Lady and St John as the representatives of a vast Cosmic glyph which existed *before* Time. Nevertheless these representatives, being aligned with the glyph *in Time*, become themselves "glyphs of the glyph".

The coming of the Cosmic Christ in the Aquarian Age, the return of the redeemed "Merlin", "Arthur", and the Arthurian Figures in the Racial spheres refer to the time when man himself will take on the remains of his karma not dealt with by the last Great Redeemer. This individual karma—be it understood the least part of the karma—must be fully realized in order that it may be abreacted. Our Lord took on himself what may be described as the "mass disbalance" of the whole Evolution and the aspects of individual sin which were clogging the Machinery of the Universe. The weight of *millions of years* of sin was, therefore, laid on the Divine Scapegoat who abreacted it in the short time we know of. This achievement shows the vast importance of realization compared with the relatively slight value of time itself. It is vitally important to understand what REALIZATION is and that it has little connection with physical plane timing. True realization in its myriad degrees of intensity implies some measure of definite abreaction of karma and the rending of the Veil between man and his Cosmic origin; this Veil was interposed in the Lemurian Age by the Lemurian Sin. Before this Sin and the differentiation of the sexes in evolution the human being consisted of the Higher Self in touch with the Divine Spark; there was no Personality as we now know it. The first "projections" from the Higher Self as we now understand them were evolved around the "Ego" created as a result of the Lemurian Shadow.

Notes on Madness, Lemurian Sin, etc.

The Aquarian attitude towards madness will be very different from the Piscean which has been accompanied by so much shame and embarrassment. It has been considered a terrible thing to have a member of the family in an asylum, but in the Aquarian Age far more people will be treated openly in mental hospitals and many will go there of their own free-will. Healing in the Aquarian Age will be more directed to mental conflicts and troubles rather than physical disease. This is connected with the beginning of the final dissolution of the separateness of the "Ego" and with the right understanding of the Ring-Chaos.[1] Madness implies a refusal to accept the reality of the Ring-Chaos as a thrust-block, and the denial of the need to accept and seek Change. It is a very severe visitation of the forces of the Holy Third Sephirah (Binah) for the forces of the Dark Mother (Ama) and of the Ring-Chaos are one. The dissolution of the Ego is the Third Birth and involves an esoteric, deliberate and fully-controlled "going out of one's mind" into the Cosmic Whole. Any refusal to accept the dissolution of the Ego will entail mental disorder for, at that stage, if the Ego is not obedient to evolutionary Law it could become so inflated that it would burst its boundaries involuntarily and out of all conscious control. It might be said that the difference between madness and the Third Birth is that in madness the Ego bursts its boundaries involuntarily, and in the Third Birth the Ego with knowledge and dedication is consciously dissolved—there is a conscious deliberate "rending of the

[1] See *The Cosmic Doctrine*.

Veil" and the adept takes up his work as an evolved part of the Greater Whole, "individual" but not "separate".

The "Lemurian Shadow" was fundamentally the "Sin of Separateness". In the beginning it was intended that evolution should proceed by the experience of differentiation as a result of the epigenetic factors in the Atoms (using the terminology of the "Cosmic Doctrine"), but the result of the Lemurian Sin was the separation of the Higher Self from the lower vehicles and physical form, having, as one of the many bad results, the loss of memory of the higher states of consciousness. The Divine Spark (or Logoidal Consciousness) could not prevent this as it cannot upon its own plane provide the formative aspect needed for manifestation. The physical plane manifestation, therefore, developed "Ego" consciousness—the consciousness of a *separate* being. If there had been "differentiation" and not "separation" the resulting consciousness would have been that of "individualization": much lies in the understanding and realization of the difference between what would have been the "individualization-consciousness" and what is the "ego-conscious ness", or "separation-consciousness". Man must eventually achieve "individualization-consciousness" in which the Divine Spark, Higher Self and Lower Self will all be in harmonious function and the consciousness of the body of Malkuth be recognized for what it really is, a cell in the body of the "Earth Mother". A basic problem of the human evolution as the result of the "Fall" is the conflict in the individual between the Elemental and Spiritual aspects of the One Life. In its severest forms this conflict leads to a kind of schizophrenia in which the Elemental life of the person becomes quite a separate existence from the spiritual.

Note. This subject is a very deep and difficult one. The language used and the ideas conveyed are as it were "approximations"; that is to say they are intended to lead to an understanding of the subject rather than to give hard and fast definitions. These remarks apply also to the *Glyph of the Crucifixion.* Generally speaking such teachings of the

Tradition are given to help the mind on to its own con-
clusions and realizations.

Pan as a Symbol.   The "Great God Pan" in the final understanding of him, is a Chokmah figure in the Solar-Logoidal
System. He is a symbol that bears relation to the symbol of
"the-Serpent-that-holds-his-tail-in-his-mouth". In the Great
God Pan lies the understanding both of the beginning and
ending of the sex-force. He represents the "rousing of
Kundalini" and he also represents that force used in the
service of the higher magic of wisdom. Yet any figure that
represents the beginning and the end conjoined is still a symbol and must eventually fade out to give place to Reality.
The *Reality* of the Great God Pan can be nothing less than
a part of the Solar Logos.

The saying "all the gods are one god and all the goddesses
are one goddess and there is one Initiator" should be
constantly worked on. The "one Initiator" is increasing
realization as a result of the increasing integration of
Higher Self and Personality which leads on to the "Empty
Room" in Daath. Therefore in varying degrees and upon
different levels all gods and goddesses represent aspects of
the One God Which is both "male" and "female".

Byron.   Non-human Forces sometimes overshadow humans
and bring in influences of other Racial Groups than that of
those humans. The various Racial Groups differ in their
influences, hence the different types of Elementals "seen" in
various countries. Byron is an illustration of one influenced
by Forces of more than one Racial Group. In addition he
had a daemonic form of "daimon" overshadowing his
Higher Self and this daimon had no opportunity in that
incarnation of manifesting save mainly through the intellect.
The revolutionary forces at work in Byron's day were able to
use this dynamic daimon to some extent but more than half
remained unexpressed. Thus there is a sense of something
"tearing itself to pieces" all the time and having to do all it
could with the utmost urgency since time was short. (The
poet died at the age of 36.)

Form (In Binah and Yesod).   Binah represents the *concept* behind Form and its Archangel represents the Intelligence behind Form, "the Formless Builder of Form" working behind both the Dark and Bright Aspects. Yesod represents the etheric mesh of Form.

Healing and the Four Elements. The Aquarian Age is specially concerned with "Air-healing" through the use of the human mind and certain Forces of Air—hence Steiner's references to the value of the mistletoe which is an Air symbol. In this Age in addition to the special Air aspect the healing values of all Four Elements should be re-established and the power of each be realized. In each Element there are harmful as well as healing Forces. The great healers of former Ages worked mainly through a certain "ray" of the Sun and upon different levels of that ray. Our Lord used this solar ray by bringing it down through himself on to others. Other solar healers used another level of this ray and brought it into contact with the patient's Higher Self whence it approached his Personality; they were not, of course, able to contact it in the major degree of force used by Our Lord.

Archetypes (refer also to previous notes). It must be remembered that Archetypes, though possessing a certain defined aspect of force, work in phases. Thus the three great Logoidal Aspects (Love, Wisdom, Power) work each in three phases. For example, the Wisdom Aspect works through Wisdom-wisdom, Wisdom-power, Wisdom-love. In the development of an initiate there may at times appear to be a retrogression to a type of manifestation which was thought to have been left behind, but what really happens is that during initiatory development each Path is retraced upon a higher arc. Thus an archetypal force may again take up the work of past years but upon a higher level. The lower curve of a new spiral of evolution corresponds with the ascending curve of the previous spiral.

The Watchman (or Watcher on the Tower) is an archetypal figure sometimes used from the Inner Planes to help the soul to realize its true destiny. It represents the eternal indestructible part of each one—linking the Higher Self with the Divine Spark. It recognizes only Reality and therefore its actions seek to destroy all that hinders realization of a soul's destiny. The temporal part of each one is ultimately destroyed because it is unrecognized by the Watchman. He is a figure of Eternity, immovable, unchanging, belonging to the Past, Present and Future, making them one. He is a Daath figure, related to the Abstract Mind and Causative Planes.

Horus is sometimes called the Lord of the Aquarian Age. He is a winged complete being containing within himself his father Osiris and his mother Isis. Isis and Osiris were one being in primeval days and later split into two. Their son represents each on the new arc—joined once more into one being. Thus Isis and Osiris represent the primal good Lemurian Age and Horus represents the completed Aquarian version of that Age raised to a spiritual level—hence the wings.

Earth-bound Souls. Earth-bound souls can, broadly, be divided into two types.

1. The type of soul who, by reason of karmic implications, has strong contact with Earth conditions.

In the phase following physical death, such a type can easily be drawn back because the "earth" vibrations are stronger than the spiritual body of the soul until after the lapse of a certain amount of time in which the spiritual body can be built up for activity on the higher and more subtle planes. This is one of the reasons why "angels" attend at a man's death—they protect him during the phase of adjustment to the new conditions, their vibrations help him to move into a "new mansion".

If the soul is drawn back it is usually due to weakness in the ethical nature, or to a swamping by the earth forces due to special evolutionary, karmic factors in which it is involved—often in relation to others who still remain on the physical plane. Such souls are always helped on the Inner Planes by more evolved human beings as well as by angels.

2. The strong type of soul who, to suit his own conveni-

ence, wills to remain as close as possible to earth conditions, refusing to undergo the subjective experiences which will build the spiritual body.

This type of soul realizes that without "a body" the forces will begin to disintegrate, to diffuse, and that this will mean destruction to his way of life. He therefore puts up a tremendous fight, causing what is known as "haunting", and can, in order to maintain himself, use obsession of animals and creatures of lower development. It is necessary for the Adepti to deal with such cases for the "will" of a man is involved. If a case were so severe that the "will" had to be broken the result would be disintegration of the human soul; the Adepti work to change the "will" if at all possible. The unpleasant, frightening and sometimes dangerous symptoms of haunting are due to the fact that by virtue of his higher grade this departed human being can, for a certain period of time—until the higher Cosmic forces have built up a wall of pressure to prevent this—manipulate and control the vibrations of the "earth" or of a lower type of being.

An Inner Plane Adept is handicapped in his work on this type of condition by not having a physical form to work with or through, because the higher forces, which are being brought down to build up the wall of pressure that will effectively seal the soul off from the earth contacts, need to be "earthed" through a physical form. Otherwise the wall, however strong, lacks roots and the earth-bound soul of great strength will overthrow it. Also, a haunting is fed by fear. For these reasons, the Adepti need in such work the strong Adept on the Physical Plane of compassionate understanding. The Adepti on the Inner Plane deal with the Cosmic forces and the Individuality of the man; the Physical Plane Adept's co-operation is needed on the lower levels of the Earth's forces and the Personality of the man involved. If properly understood, such work has regenerative effect on all who are in any way involved.

The Earth and Venus. The Earth was "incarnated" in the sphere of Venus at a very early phase. Consequently there is a contact between Venus and Earth.

Netzach has the Rose and the Lamp—two great Rosicrucian symbols—as its own, also it has the girdle or zone. Netzach has far more significance than as the sphere of "romance". Here are found three symbols used by the Rosicrucians, and here is the sphere from which the great Manu brought the three gifts to man.

The zone or girdle holds an inner significance of the Earth's contact with Venus. (The legend of the girdle of Ishtar—the last possession that the goddess was called on to surrender in the Underworld during her search for Tammuz—must have had deep spiritual meaning).

The Earth contacted deep spiritual awareness during her Venus phase and from Venus spiritual teaching came to Earth in her present phase, through the Manu Melchizedek. Among the three Netzach symbols in the Mystical Qabalah and those three gifts of the Manu there is an inner alignment of meaning though not of form; the Lamp is thus aligned with Asbestos, for only when a man can withstand spiritual Fire and Water may he hold that Lamp in his hand. This is the sphere that contains the Lamp which holds and shows forth the Flame. The Flame is drawn from Chokmah and fanned by Geburah but shown to the Earth by Netzach. Netzach is, in one tradition, the source of the Grail—the emerald which fell from Lucifer's crown as he came to Earth.

Astrology. (1). It is said that the first formative forces streamed upon the Earth from the eye of the Constellation of Taurus—associated with Aldebaran.

(2). In the earliest Lemurian days certain Adepti came to Earth from the planet Jupiter which contains a "secret scheme" connected with the Earth.

Racial Forces. In this Age, all Racial forces are undergoing changes; Racial Angels themselves are being influenced from more remote spheres by other Cosmic Beings.

When a man reincarnates, the Race to which he is sent is by no means a matter of chance, for the different lessons necessary and the different Karmic details to be worked out cannot always be found in the Race to which there may be a natural gravitation from past lives. In this fact we may find an understanding of "the traitor", the "aggressive pacifist" and such figures who have had, probably in the last incarnation, links with a Race which at that time were legitimate, but now may be out of place. The unevolved man is often swayed to some extent by his former Racial Angel. The more evolved man realizes that his duty is to his present Racial Angel but his past life may enable him to handle "enemy" force in wartime with special skill.

Races nowadays are less defined through blood: they tend to be in categories of language, blood being more and more mixed. The influences of the territory upon which a Race was first settled continue as a subconscious element however, or, to put it differently, people of the same language fall heir to the forces of the land in which the language matured. The blood-bond represents the Element of Fire, to which indeed Racial Angels also belong. The language-bond represents the Element of Air. There is much to be learnt of this in the study of the occultism of speech. As time proceeds, we shall tend to draw back to one Root-Race and Europe is now tending towards this (and Britain is included). The Russian Race tends to the East and to join up once more with the Mongolian powers via Siberia. Behind these Mongolian powers are remote forces for good working from Tibet very gradually upon Russia.

The symbolic formula of Race and Language is the Tower of Babel. This Tower was built out of time and therefore had to be destroyed. It should now be built up, for now we tend rightfully "to reach to the skies" and to have "one language".

Vanity. Apart from its more easily recognizable manifestations, vanity can be the result of a form of hate and distaste for the Personality by an "averse" aspect of a Higher Self. In such a case the Personality of early days will probably be found to have been spurned by that averse aspect and the instrument provided for incarnation refused or its experiences rejected. A kind of hate can be directed all the time by what seems to be the inner levels of the Personality against the Personality itself resulting in a slow and insidious form of suicide. Flattery or even comfort offered by others are not acceptable to this type of vanity which can consider only its own perverted reflection. Thus the perverted opinions of the false image or aspect biases all matters concerning that Self. Self love and self-hate are two sides of the same coin.

Racial Angels (See also above).

These angels are evolving somewhat like the Higher Selves of human beings and have to move on to other stages of development which in their case means working behind a different Race. As with men, the Racial Angel's main force may focus out of true alignment with its source and then very often an evil power will use the Racial Angel's force, even as an evil Personality will utilize the force of its Higher Self in wrong ways.

The Racial Angels may be compared to some extent with the Guardian Angel connected with the individual. These latter are embodiments of the Logoidal Will, split off into an entity attached to each human unit when spiritual differentiation took place. The Racial Angels are entities holding one of the especial aspects of the Manu who first guided the main branch of the Race. (Thus the Aryan Leader Rama has left aspects of his power in the various Aryan Races).

The Racial Angels—when properly evolved—earn a seat at the sidereal Round Table. Every now and again, some political measure is introduced which marks this concept. Again and again also it is found that the seat will not be taken until after a long time—even as a man cannot sit at the Round Table until he is king of himself. Angels of large and backward races are not at the same stage as Angels of the relatively developed nations. There is a lack of cohesion in such racial vehicles which are normally not welded properly with the Group-mind. In such conditions a strong and scheming party may interpolate a "false" Angel and this "false" Angel takes the place of the true Racial Guardian, which was not strongly linked up to the Group.

Where several Races are amalgamated into one, the several Racial Angels are in one aura, and this aura may be regarded as one vast Oversoul. In this way the various feline groups are included in the Oversoul or aura of the Arch-Lion, and the Earth and the present Moon are parts of one Oversoul or aura.

Uriel and Sandalphon. Uriel is the Regent of the Element of Earth, Sandalphon of the Sphere of Earth (Malkuth), and they have an interlinked relationship, each being Regent of a densest aspect of force. *Sandalphon* rules over the structure of the life-forms within this planet—thus he rules over the evolution of consciousness and of form upon the earth and so is Ruler of the "Souls of Fire", which is a symbolic name for the consciousness of the atoms. *Uriel* rules over the basic forces of the earth itself, particularly the seismic powers, and was connected with this planet before man inhabited it. He has guided earth's evolution before its form solidified when it was passing through its fiery and watery stages. He is said to have foretold the Atlantean cataclysms and to have been the teacher of Enoch. Uriel brought the great Deluge—or, at least, administered it to the earth as a server of greater Powers. Through his agency Fire, Water and Air are esoterically "permitted" to work upon earth. At one time Uriel was a Regent on the Old Moon and some of his power relates, therefore, to the Inner Earth.

The Inner Earth Potencies relate to the Old Moon (the moon which preceded the present planet) and to pre-Atlantean days when the human consciousness was somewhat of the nature of the Atziluth of Yesod. The Inner Earth is connected with a certain type of physical healing because it contains the first manifestation of the Four Elements and the primary components of the human body.

Raphael and Michael are each, at times, ascribed to the Sun. *Raphael* represents the basic forces of the Sun as he "stands within the Sun". *Michael* represents the solar forces in their aspect of spiritual power. Thus he directs one aspect of the power behind "The Solar Hero"—whether god or demi-god or human and, representing the Supernal Fire, is in charge of the guarding of the approaches to consciousness from the Infernal Fire. He is ruler over the holy Beni Elohim. An "unholy" section of these Beni Elohim helped in the Black Magic of Atlantis.

Endurance.   The esoteric concept of Endurance as a virtue is not in any way a form of the "slave mentality"; it is the force of the rocks which *cannot* be moved and full awareness of that force.

Saturn, and a note on Animals.   The "Saturn-evolution" of humanity was the Golden Age for Saturn was the first "sun" of our humanity—not the Sun-behind-the-sun, but simply the first sun. Matter was then withdrawn from that planet and used on other planes and Saturn became the "planet of Death and Constriction". (The higher arcs of the Dark Mother deal with the breaking-down and building up of the debris of universes, i.e. Chaos.)

That was Eden or the Golden Age and its symbolism holds much interest. Saturn was connected with both solar and lunar developments of very remote Ages. Its magical metal is lead; to transmute this base metal into gold is a well-known symbolical alchemical operation. The *depth* of this symbolism lies in the fact that the lead must be turned *back* into gold. There is a mention in the Cosmic Doctrine of the star Alpha Centauri, and the star 'γ' (Gamma) of that constellation was that first contacted by the Logoidal Mind when contemplating the beginning of human evolution in *form*. The higher animals are developments of Logoidal "experiments" which might have been human had not their Over-souls failed in certain points. The four highest types, however, have much part in the *design* of man—the Four Holy Living Creatures. Nevertheless, it was in the Centaur's sphere that something of the true design was reached. Hence the Centaur is a constellation of great import and the astrological equivalent if strong in a horoscope may indicate a special aptitude for the understanding of humanity. It is easy to see, also, how the deeply debased use of knowledge of these matters was a kind of evil inspiration to the Lemurian sinners.

Archetypes (see also above).   The coalescing with a Cosmic Archetype is a very significant act. It means that a spiritual concept received from the Logoidal Mind becomes an actuality in Malkuth because it is lived out. This concept is first given to humanity in the form of a myth—and a myth may be likened to a dream of the Logoidal Unconscious which then becomes translated to a projection of human consciousness. Work on an Archetype helps a soul, group, or nation to redeem and assimilate an aspect of itself which had previously either been rejected or projected. Therefore there are many kinds of Archetypes, some dealing with the Personality specifically, some with the Individuality as well as the universal and Logoidal Archetypes, which can be applied to groups and nations. It is all part of the process of integration.

Pendragon. Arthur's symbol of the Dragon refers to Lemuria when the constellation Draco held the Pole Star It becomes also either the Winged Serpent of the Higher Wisdom or the Evil Serpent.

Death, Change, Reincarnation, etc. The system of "change" —which later became "death"—was, at first, stages of withdrawal from the earth-plane, corruption of the physical vehicle had not as yet become stereotyped. The physical vehicle itself was hardly physical in the sense in which we now use the word, it was a densifying etheric vehicle which could be cast off somewhat like a complete skin which another human being could then use while the former occupant returned to phases of inner plane life till he once more contacted in realization his own origins on entry into the Solar Logoidal System—passing once more in reverse back up the path of human evolution as it then was. Such a journey, to which the incarnationary being brought its own experience and added its own quota of development, was much simpler and shorter then than it is now for we are speaking of the beginnings of human history. Now the process is a long and intricate one for after the ending by physical death of a period of development on earth the spirit of man passes on a long journey of inter-incarnationary processes in which the evolutionary phases of the Higher Self are recapitulated again through the previous chains of its development before humanity lived on the present earth. This goes on at the same time that the Personality and higher vehicles recapitulate and absorb in meditation the experiences of the incarnation just ended.

All progress follows the law of recapitulation which involves the great laws of change, transmutation and sacrifice. Physical recapitulation can be observed in the early stages of the human embryo. In the Aquarian Age Yesod is much concerned with redemption and equilibrium.

Note on the inner vehicles of man. In the "Heroic Age" (and even in later days among the Greek philosophers) the mind did not work in quite the same way as it does today. In the Heroic Age the concrete mind was certainly in use and developing but not nearly so developed as it became later. It followed that the great Archetypes and the Principles behind them worked through the *etheric* body in a manner not possible nowadays. Hence in tales of those days there can be discerned a macrocosmic grandeur in the microcosm. The concrete mind played a relatively smaller part in the make-up of man but the Abstract mind was normally in touch with the "thinker" of the day. At present the reverse is the case, for the Abstract Mind has receded in the uninitiated generally and it is the destiny of modern man to work as much as may be *through* his concrete mind. Thus everything today is necessarily seen in different perspective. Great heroism indeed does exist today but does not reflect itself, so to speak, *directly* upon the etheric from macrocosmic levels. To the modern mind, for example, the dragging of the body of Hector by Achilles after the latter had slain him seems cruel and dreadful but it is probable that even the Trojans did not take that view at the time. It was "gigantic" revenge on the grand scale of Hector and Achilles—a revenge in which the Oversouls of both Greeks and Trojans took part. Thus is drama born or, in Mystery language, thus are rituals built and worked.

The "Masters" (see also above).

In the East—especially in India—the conditions and atmosphere are much easier to manipulate from the Inner

Planes for purposes of manifestation. Such manifestations are of the etheric or subtle aspects of matter and, being of matter, can be termed "physical" but that word has then a meaning somewhat different from what is usually understood by it. When the Theosophical Society was inaugurated the strongest possible manifestations of the Inner Plane Adepti were needed to impress the teaching, but when that had been achieved the same strength of manifestation was no longer called for.

Concerning the "incarnations" of Inner Plane Adepti, the question is more complex than usually thought and there are differences between the degrees of incarnation. A suitable disciple of a certain Master can be used by that Master, with the consent and co-operation of the Higher Self of that disciple, for a type of incarnation and the result would differ little from a genuine incarnation for as long as the Master's purpose required. The incarnating Force, however, would be so incarnated only temporarily and intermittently and the Personality thus manifesting it would not be its own true Projection. An example of this on the very highest level is said to be the manifestation during three years of an aspect of the Christ in the Lord Jesus in order to accomplish a great work, the high initiate who manifested the Force having had other lives on earth directed by his own Spirit.

The Archangel Sandalphon
This Archangel is the guide of the planet Earth—the Regent of Malkuth (see Cosmic Doctrine). He has guided Earth since Lemurian days and many of his relations with Earth figure in mythologies and the myths of certain gods. His development affects humanity somewhat as the evolution of humanity affects the development of the Earth (the Planetary Spirit as described in the Cosmic Doctrine). The Racial Angels are in his especial jurisdiction and certain countries and their influences are in a deep sense the result of his own stages of growth.

Pallas Athene. Wisdom is virgin and unadulterated: to some extent it is veiled for the world could not survive the sight of it naked: the deeper into matter it penetrates the more must it be shielded, and therefore it is armed for its own protection: it wears a helmet in order that its own fire shall not destroy the brain: it is begotten, not made: it is born of the Father, i.e. the Divine Spark through Logoidal contact: it bears the spear and holds all knowledge. In short it is Pallas Athene and on her shield is the Gorgon's Head, veiled or unveiled.

INDEX

THE SOCIETY OF THE INNER LIGHT

The Society of the Inner Light is a Society for the study of Occultism, Mysticism, and Esoteric Psychology and the development of their practice.

Its aims are Christian and its methods are Western.

Students who, after due inquiry, desire to pursue their studies further, may take the Correspondence Course. Their training will be in the theory of Esoteric Science, and they will be given the discipling which prepares for its practice.

For further details apply for a copy of the WORK & AIMS of the Society from:

> The Secretariat
> The Society of the Inner Light
> 38 Steele's Road
> London NW3 4RG
> England

THE INNER LIGHT JOURNAL, a quarterly magazine, founded by Dion Fortune, is devoted to the study of Mysticism, Esoteric Christianity, Occult Science and the Psychology of Superconsciousness. Inquire with the Society at the address above for subscription rates.

Dion Fortune (1891–1946), founder of The Society of the Inner Light, is recognized as one of the most luminous and significant figures of 20th-century esoteric thought. A prolific writer, pioneer psychologist, and powerful psychic, she dedicated her life to the revival of the Mystery Tradition of the West. She left behind a solidly established system of teaching and a school of initiation based on her knowledge of many systems, ancient and modern. Her books were published before World War II, and have been continuously in demand since that time.